JUICE

JUICE

over **100 nutritious** juices
& smoothies to **rehydrate,**
soothe & energize

LOVE FOOD™

This edition published by Parragon Books Ltd in 2016
LOVE FOOD is an imprint of Parragon Books Ltd

Parragon Books Ltd
Chartist House
15–17 Trim Street
Bath BA1 1HA, UK
www.parragon.com/lovefood

ISBN 978-1-4748-1752-3

Printed in China

Introduction by Fiona Hunter
New recipes by Jane Hughes
New photography by Tony Briscoe and Al Richardson
Production by Fiona Rhys-Griffith
Designed by Beth Kalynka

Notes for the Reader
This book uses both metric and imperial measurements. Follow the same units of measurement throughout; do not mix metric and imperial. All spoon measurements are level: teaspoons are assumed to be 5 ml, and tablespoons are assumed to be 15 ml. Unless otherwise stated, milk is assumed to be full fat, eggs and individual fruits and vegetables are medium, pepper is freshly ground black pepper and salt is table salt. Unless otherwise stated, all root vegetables should be peeled prior to using.

The times given are an approximate guide only. Preparation times differ according to the techniques used by different people and the cooking times may also vary from those given.

Please note that any ingredients stated as being optional are not included in the nutritional values provided. The nutritional values given are approximate and provided as a guideline only, they do not account for individual cooks, scales and portion sizes. The nutritional values provided are per serving or per item.

While the publisher of the book and the original author(s) of the recipes and other text have made all reasonable efforts to ensure that the information contained in this book is accurate and up to date at the time of publication, anyone reading this book should note the following important points: -

Medical and pharmaceutical knowledge is constantly changing and the author(s) and the publisher cannot and do not guarantee the accuracy or appropriateness of the contents of this book;
In any event, this book is not intended to be, and should not be relied upon, as a substitute for appropriate, tailored professional advice. Both the author(s) and the publisher strongly recommend that a doctor or other healthcare professional is consulted before embarking on major dietary changes;
For the reasons set out above, and to the fullest extent permitted by law, the author(s) and publisher: (i) cannot and do not accept any legal duty of care or responsibility in relation to the accuracy or appropriateness of the contents of this book, even where expressed as 'advice' or using other words to this effect; and (ii) disclaim any liability, loss, damage or risk that may be claimed or incurred as a consequence – directly or indirectly – of the use and/or application of any of the contents of this book.

JUICE

You may think it's rare to find a topic on which nutritionists agree but there is one subject where there is no argument – the fact that most of us don't eat nearly enough fruit and vegetables. Getting your daily dose of vitamins from natural sources, such as fruit and vegetables, is a much better idea than relying on expensive dietary supplements – not only do they taste better but nutritionists believe that fruit and vegetables contain a variety of other compounds, known as phytochemicals which help us stay healthy and disease free.

The benefits of eating a diet rich in fruit and vegetables is well documented – it can reduce the risk of a whole host of medical conditions including heart disease, stroke, certain types of cancer, cataracts, high blood pressure, dementia and Alzheimer's disease. But the benefits don't end there – studies show that people who eat plenty of fruit and vegetables have fewer wrinkles and skin that looks more youthful.

Although most of us are aware of the five-a-day message, few of us manage to reach the target. Even people who enjoy eating fruit and vegetables can find it a struggle and for those who don't like fruit or veg it can seem like an impossible target. Juices and smoothies offer the perfect solution to this problem. They are quick and easy to make and the whole family will love them.

Drink your Way to Health & Vitality

Juices like Vegetable Belly Treat are a great way to disguise vegetables, so that even the most reluctant vegetable eater can enjoy them. Variety may be the spice of life but it's also a vital ingredient in a healthy balanced diet and it's particularly important when it comes to fruit and vegetables because different fruit and vegetables contain different phytochemicals which work together to keep us healthy in different ways.

Juices and smoothies are a great way to expand the variety of fruit and vegetables in your diet. In this book you'll find juices like Beat the Morning Blues which have been designed to boost energy and give you a healthy boost of good nutrition to start the day, others like Up the Anti and Green Goddess will help to nourish and boost immunity. Other chapters focus on drinks which will help soothe, hydrate or detox your body. Whatever your reason for juicing or making a smoothie, this book provides plenty of options that are not just healthy but delicious too!

Juices vs Smoothies

What's the Difference?

Although in many ways juices and smoothies are very similar – both are quick and easy to make, truly delicious and packed with vitamins and minerals – there are also important differences between the two.

Juices are made by squeezing the liquid from fruit and/or vegetables. Much of the fibre is left behind when you make juice which means your body doesn't have to work so hard to digest juices and the nutrients are absorbed quickly into the blood stream.

Smoothies are made by blending fruit and/or vegetables with other ingredients like milk, yogurt, nuts or fruit juice. If you want to avoid dairy you can use dairy-free alternatives like rice, oat, soya or almond milk.

What Equipment Do I Need?

If you plan to make both smoothies and juices you'll need to buy two separate machines. For smoothies you'll need a smoothie maker or blender but to make juices you'll need a juice extractor.

The most basic juicer you can buy is an electronic citrus press because they are compact and easy to clean but they will only juice citrus fruits. To juice other fruit and vegetables you will need to buy a juice extractor.

Before you invest in a juicer it is worth thinking about how serious you are about juicing, how often you plan to use your juicer and where you're going to store it. If you have the space on your work surface and are serious about juicing, a masticating model is a good choice.

Masticating juicers crush the fruit and vegetables and then push the juice out through a mesh wire. They tend to be heavier and more expensive than centrifugal juicers but they do produce a larger quantity of juice and retain more nutrients. If you want to juice wheatgrass this is the type of juicer you will need to.

Centrifugal juicers are usually smaller and lighter so easier to store but they can be noisy. Fruit and vegetables are fed via a tube onto a fast spinning metal filter with grating teeth. The juice and the pulp are separated by centrifugal force. Centrifugal juicers spin fast, which can introduce more oxygen and heat into the juice, whereas masticating models are much gentler.

With juicers you definitely get what you pay for and if you're serious about juicing it's worth investing in the most sophisticated machine you can afford. If you're planning to make large quantities of juice in one go, choose a model that ejects pulp into a separate compartment, so you won't have to keep stopping to empty out the pulp.

What Ingredients Can I Use?

You can use almost any raw fruit, vegetables or herbs to make juice and once the juice is made you can add in extras like spirulina powder. When you make juice, the juice is separated from the fibre but of course you can always add some of the pulp/fibre back into the juice before you drink it. Some juices, especially the green vegetables, can be an acquired taste, but apple, carrot, red pepper and citrus fruits are usually an instant success.

Stick to fruit and vegetables that are in season. Choose ripe but not over ripe fruit, avoid bruised or wilted produce and whenever possible buy organic. Using a variety of different fruit and vegetables, or combining one or two in the same juice, will help ensure that you get the full range of nutrients.

Smoothies offer more versatility and in fact the possibilities are endless. You can use fresh, frozen, canned or dried fruit or vegetables and blend them with milk, yogurt, dairy-free milk alternatives, nuts and seeds, nut butters and protein powders.

Frozen and canned fruit in smoothies make a good alternative to fresh fruit, especially in the winter months when fresh fruit can be more expensive. Using frozen fruit gives smoothies a thick creamy consistency and helps them stay cold for longer, which is useful if you are not going to drink them straight away.

Ready-to-eat dried fruits such as apricots, prunes and dates can also be used to make smoothies – to make the fruit soft enough to puree you'll need to soak it in fruit juice overnight. Levels of vitamins and some phytochemicals diminish during storage so to minimise these losses buy little and often.

Give Me Some Top Tips!

- Prepare fruit and vegetables just before juicing. Wash thoroughly, scrubbing tough skinned varieties with a soft brush before juicing.

- Make sure all your fruit and vegetables are chopped as necessary into similar sizes; soft fruit such as bananas, can be in larger chunks, while hard items like carrots, should be chopped small. Always use the provided plunger for feeding items into a juicer. Don't try to blend without adding liquid – put solids into a blender bowl and add liquid.

- It's always best to drink freshly prepared juice as even when it's stored in the fridge it can turn brown, which shows the nutrients are oxidising. Cold-pressed juices tend to store well for longer (24 hours or more), if kept in the refrigerator.

- You can boost the nutritional value of juices and smoothies by adding other ingredients like chia seeds, wheat germ, nuts and seeds, or tahini. Try to avoid adding too much sugar.

- Keep any storecupboard supplements fresh. Pay attention to any expiration dates and discard out-of date items. Store all items in a dry, dark and preferably cool place, in a sealed container. Always keep liquid supplements in the refrigerator.

- The pulp that remains when you've made the juice is a good source of fibre and contains vitamins and phytochemicals so don't waste it. It can be used to thicken soup or in baking.

Whether it's to help you get the best start to the day, fuel you through a gruelling workout, or just to avoid the afternoon slump at work, finding a healthy way to get a quick and easy energy boost is essential. These recipes are packed with energy-giving ingredients and they are delicious too! Try our Berry Kick-start, Turbo Express or Muesli Motivator.

ENERGY

Power Gulp

Serves: 1 | Prep: 10–15 mins | Cook: none

Per serving: 471 KCALS | 13.8G FAT | 1.2G SAT FAT | 85G CARBS | 63.4G SUGAR | 18.9G FIBRE | 11.6G PROTEIN | 0.4G SALT

Beetroot is the favourite vegetable among sportsmen and sportswomen. It's great for boosting stamina and making muscles work harder, and is packed with vitamins, minerals, carbohydrates, protein and powerful antioxidants.

Ingredients

2 beetroots, halved
30 g/1 oz linseeds
4 plums, quartered and stoned
150 g/5½ oz seedless red grapes
225 ml/8 fl oz chilled water
crushed ice, to serve (optional)

1. Feed the beetroots through a juicer.

2. Put the linseeds into a blender and whizz until finely ground. Add the beetroot juice, plums, grapes and water and blend until smooth.

3. Pour into a glass, add crushed ice, if using, and serve immediately.

Single Shot Sports Boosters

Serves: 1 | Prep: 20 mins | Cook: none

Have one of these potent juices just before you start strenuous exercise for a vitamin and mineral boost to energize muscles and aid performance. Prepare the boosters in advance and take to the gym in a well-sealed insulated sports flask.

Per serving: 86 KCALS | 0.3G FAT | TRACE SAT FAT | 19.1G CARBS | 13.5G SUGAR | 5.6G FIBRE | 3.2G PROTEIN | 0.4G SALT

Beetroot booster

2 beetroots, halved
4 tbsp chilled water (optional)

1. To make the beetroot booster, feed the beetroots through a juicer. Pour into a glass, top up with the water, if using, and serve.

Per serving: 84 KCALS | 0.7G FAT | TRACE SAT FAT | 20.2G CARBS | 12.4G SUGAR | 4.1G FIBRE | 1.6G PROTEIN | TRACE SALT

Kiwi fruit booster

2 kiwi fruits, peeled and roughly chopped

1. To make the kiwi fruit booster, feed the kiwi fruits through a juicer. Pour into a glass and serve.

Per serving: 86 KCALS | 0.5G FAT | TRACE SAT FAT | 21.7G CARBS | 14.9G SUGAR | 3.6G FIBRE | 1.1G PROTEIN | TRACE SALT

Blueberry booster

150 g/5½ oz blueberries
4 tbsp chilled water

1. To make the blueberry booster, put the blueberries and water into a blender and blend until smooth. Pour into a glass and serve.

Sweet beetroot

Beetroot has one of the highest sugar levels of any vegetable, with the equivalent of 1 teaspoon of natural fruit sugar in each 115 g/4 oz portion, so it gives a great energy boost. It also contains folates, vitamin C and potassium, which help regulate blood pressure and nerve function.

Tropical Watermelon Wonder

Serves: 2 | Prep: 15 mins | Cook: none

Per serving: 528 KCALS | 39.7G FAT | 34.7G SAT FAT | 47.5G CARBS | 26.3G SUGAR | 6G FIBRE | 6.5G PROTEIN | TRACE SALT

Delicious watermelon is the ultimate in thirst-quenching fruits. Blending it with the tropical flavours of banana and coconut cream will give you a refreshingly exotic-tasting energy boost after a workout.

Ingredients

1 watermelon wedge, weighing about 600 g/1 lb 5 oz, peeled, deseeded and roughly chopped

2 small bananas, peeled and roughly chopped

225 ml/8 fl oz coconut cream

1. Put the watermelon, bananas and coconut cream into a blender and process until combined.

2. Pour into chilled glasses and serve.

Red Pep-up

Serves: 1 | Prep: 15 mins | Cook: none

Per serving: 93 KCALS | 0.5G FAT | TRACE SAT FAT | 21.9G CARBS | 10.9G SUGAR | 1.5G FIBRE | 2.6G PROTEIN | 0.2G SALT

Full of disease-fighting, anti-ageing antioxidants, this drink provides lots of energy from its natural sweetness to help you get through the day.

Ingredients

2 fennel bulbs with fronds, halved
1 apple, halved
1 small red pepper, halved
1 carrot, halved

1. Remove a few fronds from the fennel and reserve.

2. Feed the apple, then the fennel and red pepper, then the carrot through a juicer.

3. Pour into a glass, garnish with the reserved fennel fronds and serve.

Why not try?

Agave syrup and brown rice syrup can be used instead of honey. Agave syrup is naturally sweeter than honey. Brown rice syrup has a mild caramel flavour and is similar to maple syrup.

Berry Kick-start

Serves: 1 | Prep: 10–15 mins | Cook: none

Per serving:	288 KCALS | 5.6G FAT | 3.1G SAT FAT | 57.9G CARBS | 40.5G SUGAR | 9.5G FIBRE | 6.9G PROTEIN | 0.1G SALT

This energizing, gorgeous-looking smoothie is chock full of fresh berries and is a delicious and healthy way to kick-start your day.

Ingredients

175 g/6 oz blueberries
115 g/4 oz cranberries
150 ml/5 fl oz natural yogurt
2 tsp clear honey
4 tbsp chilled water

1. Put the blueberries and cranberries into a blender and blend.

2. Add the yogurt, honey and water and blend again until smooth.

3. Pour into a glass and serve.

Blueberry Blast

Serves: 1 | Prep: 10–15 mins | Cook: none

Per serving: 346 KCALS | 8.2G FAT | 4G SAT FAT | 62.4G CARBS | 37G SUGAR | 6.8G FIBRE | 12.1G PROTEIN | 0.2G SALT

The blueberry is a superhero in the food world. When mixed with pear, natural yogurt and chilled water, it will get you through the most hectic of schedules. You can use two apples instead of the water; just juice them with the pear.

Ingredients

1 pear, halved
115 g/4 oz blueberries
175 ml/6 fl oz natural yogurt
20 g/¾ oz wheat germ
175 ml/6 fl oz chilled water
small handful of crushed ice (optional)

1. Feed the pear through a juicer.

2. Pour the juice into a blender, add the blueberries, yogurt, wheat germ and water and blend until smooth. Add the crushed ice, if using, and blend again until smooth.

3. Pour into a glass and serve immediately.

Blueberries: good mood food

The antioxidant power of blueberries has been shown to help stabilize brain function and protect the neural tissue from oxidative stress – which may improve memory and learning and reduce symptoms of depression.

Fennel

The European plant fennel is a valuable source of vitamin B6, playing a vital part in energy metabolism. This aids the break down of carbohydrates and proteins into glucose and amino acids, used for energy in the body. This also positively impacts upon skin and hair health, whilst decreasing the risks of heart disease and diabetes.

Turbo Express
Pink Energy

Pink Energy

Serves: 1 | Prep: 15–20 mins | Cook: none

Per serving: 294 KCALS | 5.2G FAT | 0.9G SAT FAT | 56.8G CARBS | 35.9G SUGAR | 10.1G FIBRE | 10.5G PROTEIN | 0.1G SALT

Ingredients

½ papaya, peeled, deseeded and roughly chopped

150 g/5½ oz strawberries, hulled

1 banana, peeled and roughly chopped

juice of ½ lime

225 ml/8 fl oz unsweetened rice, almond or soya milk

small handful of crushed ice (optional)

1. Put the papaya, strawberries and banana into a blender and blend until smooth.

2. Add the lime juice and milk and blend again. Add the crushed ice, if using, and blend again until smooth.

3. Pour into a glass and serve.

Turbo Express

Serves: 1 | Prep: 15–20 mins | Cook: none

Per serving: 338 KCALS | 3.4G FAT | 0.7G SAT FAT | 76.2G CARBS | 54.7G SUGAR | 8.4G FIBRE | 8.1G PROTEIN | 0.1G SALT

Ingredients

¼ honeydew melon, deseeded, peeled and roughly chopped

1 banana, peeled and roughly chopped

1 kiwi fruit, peeled and roughly chopped

115 g/4 oz seedless green grapes

small handful of watercress (optional)

125 ml/4 fl oz unsweetened rice, almond or soya milk

small handful of crushed ice (optional)

1. Put the melon, banana, kiwi fruit, grapes and watercress, if using, in a blender and blend well until smooth.

2. Add the milk and crushed ice, if using, and blend again until smooth.

3. Pour into a glass and serve immediately.

Juicing oranges

Oranges vary hugely in the amount of juice that they produce. If they are kept at room temperature they will be easier to squeeze.
Adjust the thickness of this juice with water as needed.

Raspberry Rejuvenator

Serves: 1 | Prep: 15 mins | Cook: none

Per serving: 348 KCALS | 3.1G FAT | 0.1G SAT FAT | 80.4G CARBS | 54.2G SUGAR | 13.5G FIBRE | 4.6G PROTEIN | TRACE SALT

Raspberries and bananas are a delicious combination. They give the body a slowly released energy boost to re-energize you in a sustained way.

Ingredients

30 g/1 oz goji berries

1 small banana, peeled and roughly chopped

115 g/4 oz raspberries

juice of 2 oranges

small handful of crushed ice (optional)

chilled water, to taste

1. Put the goji berries in a blender and whizz until finely ground.

2. Add the banana, raspberries and orange juice and blend until smooth. Add the crushed ice, if using, and blend again until smooth.

3. Add water to taste, pour into a glass and serve immediately.

Peach Energizer

Serves: 1 | Prep: 15–20 mins | Cook: none

Per serving: 266 KCALS | 8.9G FAT | 1.1G SAT FAT | 46.8G CARBS | 35.6G SUGAR | 4.7G FIBRE | 5.4G PROTEIN | 0.1G SALT

The grapefruit blast in this drink will perk you up and sharpen your senses, while the peach will provide natural sugars to boost your energy levels and the ginger will soothe and comfort.

Ingredients

1 pink or ruby grapefruit, zest and a little pith removed, halved

1 carrot, halved

1-cm/½-inch piece fresh ginger, peeled

1 large peach, stoned and roughly chopped

1 tbsp light tahini

125 ml/4 fl oz chilled water (optional)

small handful of crushed ice

1. Feed the grapefruit, then the carrot and ginger through a juicer.

2. Pour the juice into a blender, add the peach, tahini, water, if using, and crushed ice and blend until smooth.

3. Pour into a glass and serve immediately.

Vegan Power Shake

Serves: 2 | Prep: 10–15 mins | Cook: none

Per serving: 245 KCALS | 16.9G FAT | 2.1G SAT FAT | 18.1G CARBS | 10.4G SUGAR | 2.8G FIBRE | 6.5G PROTEIN | TRACE SALT

This is a great milkshake for anyone who is vegan or lactose intolerant. Banana and maple syrup blend with the milk to make a deliciously creamy, potassium-rich shake.

Ingredients

1 large banana, peeled and roughly chopped

350 ml/12 fl oz chilled soya milk

2 tbsp vegan omega 369 oil

1 tsp maple syrup

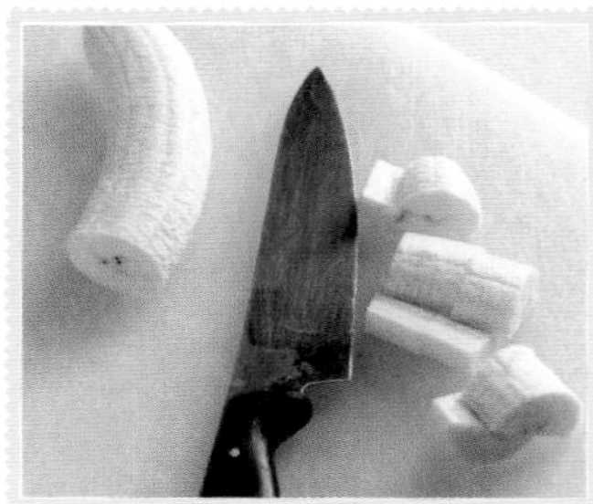

1. Put the banana into a blender with the milk and omega oil.

2. Blend gently until thoroughly combined. Add maple syrup to taste.

3. Serve immediately in tall drinking glasses.

Brilliant bananas

Naturally rich in fruit sugar and starch, bananas are great energy-boosting foods and have a high amount of potassium. They can help regulate blood pressure and may reduce the risk of heart attacks, strokes and cancer.

Muesli Motivator

Serves: 1 | Prep: 15 mins | Cook: none

Per serving:	450 KCALS | 18.5G FAT | 1.4G SAT FAT | 65.1G CARBS | 31.5G SUGAR | 16.6G FIBRE | 12.8G PROTEIN | TRACE SALT

Refreshing and super-zingy, this smoothie makes a delicious energy-packed breakfast. The natural fruit sugars and slow-release complex carbs from the grapefruit pith, oats and almonds will keep you feeling full until lunchtime.

Ingredients

20 g/¾ oz porridge oats

30 g/1 oz flaked almonds

½ ruby red grapefruit, zest and a little pith removed, deseeded and roughly chopped

150 g/5½ oz raspberries

juice of 2 oranges

125 ml/4 fl oz chilled water

1. Put the oats and almonds in a blender and blend until finely ground.

2. Add the grapefruit, raspberries, orange juice and water and blend until smooth.

3. Pour into a glass and serve.

Make it perfect!

Be sure to cut grapefruit into small pieces before putting it in the blender so that you get a smooth juice.

Almond Butter & Raspberry Bliss

Serves: 2 | Prep: 10 mins | Cook: none

Per serving: 338KCALS | 14.1G FAT | 1G SAT FAT | 28.4G CARBS | 11.6G SUGAR | 10.7G FIBRE | 6.7G PROTEIN | 0.2G SALT

If you don't usually eat breakfast, try this smoothie. It is a really quick and tasty, nutrient-packed start to a busy day.

Ingredients

1 banana, peeled and roughly chopped
200 g/7 oz raspberries
400 ml/14 fl oz unsweetened almond milk
40 g/1½ oz almond butter
4 tsp stevia granules
2 tsp vanilla extract
ice cubes

1. Put the banana in a blender with the raspberries.

2. Add the almond milk, almond butter, stevia granules and vanilla extract. Top up with ice cubes.

3. Blend until smooth. Drink immediately or chill overnight.

Mango for energy

A mango is 14 per cent natural sugar, and this can be quickly converted into energy by the body. It is also rich in beta-carotene and vitamin C.

Tropical Energizer

Serves: 1 | Prep: 15–20 mins | Cook: none

Per serving: 394 KCALS | 6.7G FAT | 0.9G SAT FAT | 70.4G CARBS | 47.5G SUGAR | 9.1G FIBRE | 7.6G PROTEIN | TRACE SALT

Papaya and mango are both rich in natural fruit sugars, which give an energy boost. They're also easy to digest and gentle on the stomach.

Ingredients

1 banana, peeled and roughly chopped

½ papaya, peeled, deseeded and roughly chopped

½ mango, stoned, peeled and roughly chopped

juice of 1 lime

2-cm/¾-inch piece fresh ginger, peeled and finely grated

2 tsp hemp oil

125 ml/4 fl oz unsweetened rice, almond or soya milk

small handful of crushed ice

1. Put the chopped banana, papaya and mango in a blender and blend until smooth.

2. Add the lime, ginger, oil, milk and crushed ice and blend again.

3. Pour into a glass and serve immediately.

Almonds

Almonds are rich in healthy monounsaturated fatty acids, the good kind of fat that contributes to increased heart health and lower cholesterol levels. The slow digestive process of almonds and their stack of nutrients, such as biotin and manganese, produce a more sustained type of energy in the body, leaving you feeling fuller and more alert for a longer period of time.

Banana Breakfast Wake-up

Serves: 2 | Prep: 5 mins | Cook: none

Per serving: 259 KCALS | 3.8G FAT | 0.7G SAT FAT | 55.7G CARBS | 34.4G SUGAR | 6G FIBRE | 8.3G PROTEIN | TRACE SALT

A speedy, sustaining breakfast-in-a-glass, this delicious shake is perfect for those days when time is short and you need long-lasting energy.

Ingredients

2 large ripe bananas, peeled and roughly chopped

2 tbsp oat bran

2 tbsp honey

1 tbsp lemon juice

300 ml/10 fl oz soya milk

ground cinnamon, to serve (optional)

1. Put all the ingredients in a blender and blend until smooth.

2. Pour into tall glasses, sprinkle with ground cinnamon, if using, and serve immediately.

Honey goodness

Honey supplies energy in the form of simple carbohydrates and is a mixture of fructose and glucose. The clearer the honey, the higher the level of fructose. Sweet foods stimulate the brain to produce endorphins, the body's natural painkillers.

Strawberry & Vanilla Delight

Serves: 2 | Prep: 10–15 mins | Cook: none

Per serving: 151 KCALS | 2.8G FAT | 0.3G SAT FAT | 24.6G CARBS | 16.7G SUGAR | 0.8G FIBRE | 4.7G PROTEIN | TRACE SALT

This creamy soya shake makes a great quick breakfast, or you could drink it as an instant energy boost at any time of day. Replace the soya milk with unsweetened almond milk for a subtle difference in flavour.

Ingredients

200 g/7 oz strawberries
200 ml/7 fl oz plain soya yogurt
100 ml/3½ fl oz chilled soya milk
2 tsp vanilla extract

1. Pick over the strawberries, then hull and halve them and place them in a small bowl.

2. Place the strawberry halves, yogurt, milk and vanilla extract in a blender and gently blend until thoroughly combined.

3. Serve immediately in tall drinking glasses.

Raw Cacao Milkshake

Serves: 4 | Prep: 10 mins | Cook: none

Per serving: 198 KCALS | 10.8G FAT | 2G SAT FAT | 24.9G CARBS | 15.5G SUGAR | 3.9G FIBRE | 5.2G PROTEIN | 0.1G SALT

Great for waking up your taste buds first thing, or for a nutritious chocolate hit at any time, this delicious dairy-free and gluten-free milkshake provides a perfect pick-me-up that is suitable for vegetarians and vegans too.

Ingredients

400 ml/14 fl oz almond milk
85 g/3 oz dried dates
85 g/3 oz cashew nuts
2 tbsp raw cacao powder
1 tsp ground cinnamon
handful of ice cubes
1 tbsp orange zest, to decorate

1. Place the almond milk, dates, nuts, cacao powder, cinnamon and ice in a blender.

2. Blend thoroughly until the milkshake has a thick pouring consistency.

3. Pour into chilled glasses, decorate with the orange zest and serve.

Raw cacao

Raw cacao is naturally high in antioxidants, magnesium, iron and fibre. It helps protect the nervous system and lowers blood pressure and it can also aid in reducing the risk of nerve damage, cardiovascular disease, diabetes and stroke.

Blueberry Thrill

Serves: 2 | Prep: 10 mins | Cook: none

Per serving: 85 KCALS | 2.7G FAT | 1.8G SAT FAT | 11.3G CARBS | 8.3G SUGAR | 1.3G FIBRE | 5G PROTEIN | TRACE SALT

Blueberries have long been regarded as one of nature's superfoods, and they're delicious, too. The blueberry season is very short, but this easy smoothie uses frozen blueberries, available all year round.

Ingredients

100 ml/3½ fl oz Greek-style yogurt
100 ml/3½ fl oz water
125 g/4½ oz frozen blueberries
2 whole frozen blueberries, to decorate

1. Put the yogurt, water and blueberries into a blender and blend until smooth.

2. Pour into glasses, top each with a whole frozen blueberry and serve.

We've compiled our favourite thirst-quenching drinks that are not only rehydrating but are also made from totally natural and nutritious ingredients. For hot summer days, post-exercise cool-downs or any time you fancy a refreshing juice, turn to recipes like our Summer Corn Quencher, Citrus Cleanser, Lettuce Elixir or Kale Green Tropic.

REHYDRATE

How to juice herbs

To get the most juice from herbs, sandwich them between firmer fruit or vegetables so that their weight helps to press down on the leaves as they go through the juicer chute.

Tantalizing Tomato Refresher

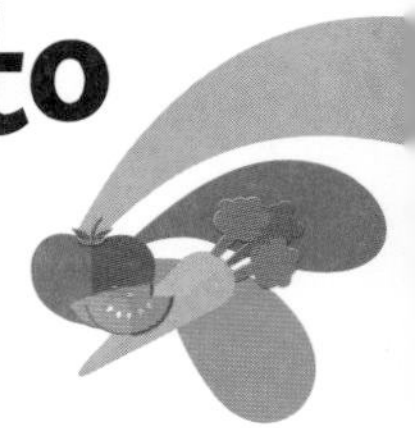

Serves: 1 | Prep: 10–15 mins | Cook: none

Per serving: 126 KCALS | 1G FAT | 0.1G SAT FAT | 27.5G CARBS | 15.7G SUGAR | 2G FIBRE | 5.2G PROTEIN | 0.3G SALT

The success of this refreshing juice depends on the quality of the tomatoes; home-grown and just-picked ones are perfect, but otherwise choose good, generously sized, deeply coloured ones sold on the vine for the best flavour.

Ingredients

2 carrots, halved
small handful of fresh basil leaves
1 celery stick, halved
2.5-cm/1-inch slice of broccoli stem
4 tomatoes
small handful of crushed ice (optional)

1. Feed the carrots, then most of the basil, the celery, broccoli and the tomatoes through a juicer.

2. Half-fill a glass with crushed ice, if using, then pour in the juice.

3. Garnish with the remaining basil leaves and serve immediately.

Cool as a Cucumber

Serves: 1 | Prep: 10–15 mins | Cook: none

Per serving: 153 KCALS | 0.9G FAT | 0.2G SAT FAT | 37.3G CARBS | 25.7G SUGAR | 1.8G FIBRE | 3.6G PROTEIN | 0.1G SALT

This is like a cooling summer salad in a glass: light and fresh, with a gentle pepperiness from the rocket, a dash of mouth-freshening garden mint and a hint of sweetness from the apple.

Ingredients

½ cucumber, halved
15 g/½ oz rocket
3 fresh mint sprigs
1 courgette
1 celery stick, halved
1 apple, halved
small handful of crushed ice (optional)
1 fresh mint sprig, to garnish

1. Feed the cucumber, rocket and mint through a juicer, followed by the courgette, celery and apple.

2. Half fill a glass with crushed ice, if using, then pour in the juice and serve immediately, garnished with a mint sprig.

Not a fan of celery?

Leave it out and add a little more cucumber instead.

Celery & Apple Revitalizer

Serves: 2 | Prep: 10–15 mins | Cook: none

Per serving: 235 KCALS | 9.9G FAT | 5.6G SAT FAT | 27.5G CARBS | 25.2G SUGAR | 2G FIBRE | 10.1G PROTEIN | 0.4G SALT

A milkshake that does you good! Celery and apple are the perfect combination in this drink, which is great on hot summer days. Serve in tall glasses with strips of celery to decorate.

Ingredients

115 g/4 oz celery, chopped
1 apple, peeled, cored and diced
600 ml/1 pint milk
pinch of sugar
salt (optional)
4 strips of celery, to garnish

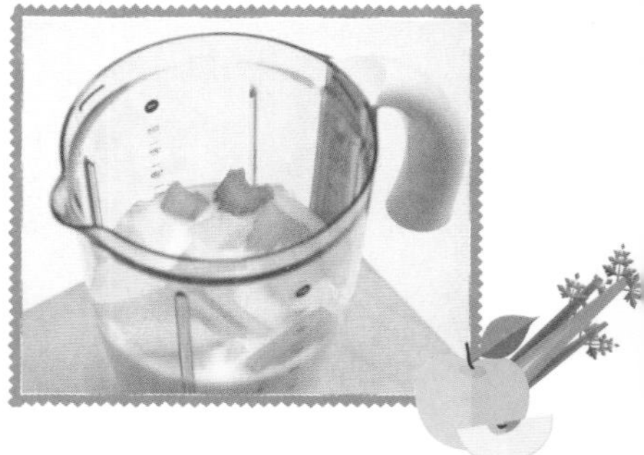

1. Place the celery, apple and milk in a blender and process until thoroughly combined.

2. Stir in the sugar and some salt, if using.

3. Pour into chilled glasses, decorate with strips of celery and serve.

Orange Refresher

Serves: 1 | Prep: 10–15 mins | Cook: none

Per serving: 131 KCALS | 0.6G FAT | 0.1G SAT FAT | 31.8G CARBS | 27.9G SUGAR | 5G FIBRE | 2.9G PROTEIN | 0.1G SALT

A glass of freshly squeezed orange juice doesn't just have to be limited to breakfast. With the addition of fresh mint and lusciously sweet melon, this rehydrating juice will refresh you at any time of the day.

Ingredients

1 orange, zest and a little pith removed, halved

1 large fresh mint sprig

200 g/7 oz cantaloupe melon, peeled and roughly chopped

1–2 fresh mint sprigs, to decorate

1. Put the orange into a food processor or blender with the mint and melon and process until smooth.

2. Pour into a glass and serve decorated with mint sprigs.

Summer Corn Quencher

Serves: 1 | Prep: 15 mins | Cook: none

Per serving: 222 KCALS | 2.1G FAT | 0.3G SAT FAT | 51.7G CARBS | 30.4G SUGAR | 2.3G FIBRE | 5.2G PROTEIN | TRACE SALT

Ingredients

1 fresh corn cob, husks and silks removed

4 fresh coriander sprigs

1 yellow pepper, deseeded and halved

1 apple, halved

small handful of crushed ice (optional)

1. Cut the niblets from the corn, then feed them through a juicer.

2. Feed the coriander, then the yellow pepper and then the apple through the juicer.

3. Half-fill a glass with crushed ice, if using, then pour in the juice and serve immediately.

Cherry Aid

Serves: 1 | Prep: 20 mins | Cook: none

Per serving: 376 KCALS | 4.8G FAT | 0.6G SAT FAT | 87.7G CARBS | 57.1G SUGAR | 4.8G FIBRE | 5.2G PROTEIN | TRACE SALT

Ingredients

2 pears, halved

1 tbsp chia seeds

175 g/6 oz cherries, stoned

125 ml/4 fl oz chilled water

small handful of crushed ice (optional)

1. Feed the pears through a juicer.

2. Put the chia seeds in a blender and whizz until finely ground. Add the pear juice, cherries, water and crushed ice, if using, and blend until smooth.

3. Pour into a glass and serve immediately.

Melon, Pear & Ginger Spritzer

Serves: 1 | Prep: 15–20 mins | Cook: none

Per serving: 247 KCALS | 0.8G FAT | 0.2G SAT FAT | 63.9G CARBS | 49.8G SUGAR | 2.2G FIBRE | 2.8G PROTEIN | 0.2G SALT

A refreshingly healthy version of ginger beer, with no chemicals and no added sugars, just 100 per cent natural ingredients.

Ingredients

½ honeydew melon, thickly sliced and peeled

1-cm/½-inch piece fresh ginger, peeled

1 pear, halved

small handful of crushed ice (optional)

125 ml/4 fl oz sparkling mineral water, chilled

1. Feed the melon, then the ginger, then the pear through a juicer.

2. Half-fill a glass with crushed ice, if using, then pour in the juice.

3. Top up with the mineral water and serve immediately.

Water versus juices

When you exercise you lose many of the minerals in your body through sweat. Water alone will rehydrate you, but so can juices. Home-made fruit and vegetable juices also boost your energy and vitamin and mineral intake and help you rehydrate more quickly, speeding up recovery time. A mixture of the two in a home-made isotonic sports drink is best.

Celery

Celery is often referred to as 'crunchy water' because of its incredible hydrating properties. Rich in minerals, just a few celery sticks can replenish levels of sodium, iron and zinc in the body. Because it aids the body's natural composition, this means that it becomes more effective in hydration than water alone, which is the reason it's also so beneficial in keeping your digestive system clear.

Kale Green Tropic

Serves: 1 | Prep: 10–15 mins | Cook: none

Per serving: 53 KCALS | 0.3G FAT | TRACE SAT FAT | 12.2G CARBS | 7.7G SUGAR | 2.2G FIBRE | 1.7G PROTEIN | TRACE SALT

Full of fresh pineapple flavour, this delicious green shot is boosted with B vitamins and essential minerals and will give you an immediate lift.

Ingredients

- 10 g/¼ oz kale, shredded
- 60 g/2¼ oz pineapple, peeled and roughly chopped
- 15 g/½ oz spinach
- ½ tsp wheatgrass powder
- 3½ tbsp chilled water
- 1 pineapple segment, to garnish

1. Put the kale and the pineapple in a blender with the spinach and wheatgrass powder.

2. Pour over the water and blend until smooth.

3. Serve immediately, garnished with the pineapple segment.

Wonderful wheatgrass

As you get used to the flavour of wheatgrass increase the amount to 1 teaspoon.

Red Pepper Reviver

Serves: 1 | Prep: 10–15 mins | Cook: none

Per serving: 100 KCALS | 10.0G FAT | 1.0G SAT FAT | 10.0G CARBS | 5.0G SUGAR | 1.0G FIBRE | 1.0G PROTEIN | TRACE SALT

This zingy juice is sure to wake you up if you're having a mid-morning snooze. Black pepper is an unexpectedly fiery spice – handle with care!

Ingredients

2 carrots, halved
2 tomatoes, halved
1 large red pepper, deseeded and halved
2 tsp lemon juice
pinch of pepper, plus extra to garnish (optional)
4–6 strips of shredded carrot, to garnish

1. Feed the carrots, then the tomatoes and red pepper through a juicer.

2. Stir in the lemon juice and pepper.

3. Pour into a glass, garnish with the strips of shredded carrot and pepper, if using, and serve.

Thumbs up for tomatoes

Tomatoes contain 90 per cent water, so are great for rehydration. They are rich in lycopene, a carotenoid pigment that turns them red. It is thought this may help prevent some forms of cancer. They are also a good source of potassium, with smaller amounts of vitamins C and E.

Citrus Cleanser

Serves: 1 | Prep: 15 mins | Cook: none

Per serving: 288 KCALS | 0.8G FAT | TRACE SAT FAT | 75G CARBS | 53.2G SUGAR | 3.3G FIBRE | 3.8G PROTEIN | TRACE SALT

Citrus fruits stimulate the digestive system. In traditional folk medicine it was thought that they also acted as a cleanser and astringent, stimulating the liver and gall bladder to function properly.

Ingredients

1 pink or ruby grapefruit, zest and a little pith removed, halved

1 orange, zest and a little pith removed, halved

1 lime, zest and pith removed from half

1 large pear, halved

small handful of crushed ice (optional)

1. Feed the grapefruit, orange, lime, and then the pear through a juicer.

2. Half-fill a glass with crushed ice, if using, then pour in the juice and serve immediately.

Grapefruit nutrition

Grapefruit is a great source of vitamin C. It is also packed with flavonoids (natural chemical compounds that may reduce early damage to DNA and cell membranes).

Red Reviver

Serves: 1 | Prep: 10 mins | Cook: none

Per serving: 200 KCALS | 0.6G FAT | TRACE SAT FAT | 50.2G CARBS | 30.8G SUGAR | 11.6G FIBRE | 3.8G PROTEIN | 0.4G SALT

The naturally sweet flavour of this deliciously vibrant red pick-me-up could be overwhelming, but it is subtly cut with tangy lime and spicy ginger.

Ingredients

2 small beetroots, halved

1 carrot, halved

1 pear, halved

½ lime, zest and pith removed, deseeded and roughly chopped

2.5-cm/1-inch piece fresh ginger, peeled

1. Put the beetroots and carrot into a blender and blend until smooth.

2. Add the pear, lime and ginger and blend again until smooth.

3. Pour into a glass and serve.

Lettuce Elixir

Serves: 1 | Prep: 10–15 mins | Cook: none

Per serving: 157 KCALS | 1.2G FAT | 0.1G SAT FAT | 35.8G CARBS | 23.6G SUGAR | 2.7G FIBRE | 5G PROTEIN | 0.5G SALT

Lettuce, celery and apple all have a high water content, so they are useful in helping the body to flush out toxins. This cleansing drink also tastes delicious!

Ingredients

100 g/3½ oz cos lettuce, roughly chopped
4 celery sticks, roughly chopped
1 green apple, halved
30 g/1 oz fresh flat-leaf parsley
1 tsp spirulina powder
1 cos lettuce leaf, to garnish
crushed ice, to serve

1. Feed the lettuce, celery and apple through a juicer with the parsley.

2. Stir through the spirulina powder until combined.

3. Pour over crushed ice, if using, and serve immediately, garnished with the lettuce leaf.

Raspberry & Watermelon Crush

Serves: 1 | Prep: 15–20 mins | Cook: none

Per serving: 125 KCALS | 1G FAT | TRACE SAT FAT | 30.6G CARBS | 17.8G SUGAR | 8.4G FIBRE | 2.7G PROTEIN | TRACE SALT

As the name suggests, watermelon is packed full of water, so what better way to rehydrate your body than with this delicately flavoured smoothie blended with the natural sweetness of raspberries and a hint of tangy lime?

Ingredients

¼ small watermelon, peeled, roughly chopped and most of the black seeds removed

½ lime, zest and most of the pith removed, deseeded and roughly chopped

115 g/4 oz raspberries

small handful of crushed ice

1. Put the watermelon and lime in a blender and blend until smooth.
2. Add the raspberries and crushed ice and blend again.
3. Pour into a glass and serve immediately.

Cut down on caffeine

Most of us drink far too much caffeine-loaded tea and coffee. Instead of quenching your thirst, these can lead to dehydration and reduce your stimulus to drink. Start choosing healthy, rehydrating juices and you will see a difference. They not only boost fluid levels but offer a nutrient hit at the same time.

Pink Zinger

Serves: 1 | Prep: 10–15 mins | Cook: none

Per serving: 166 KCALS | 0.6G FAT | TRACE SAT FAT | 43.5G CARBS | 31.7G SUGAR | 8G FIBRE | 3.5G PROTEIN | TRACE SALT

This pink citrus cleanser will tantalize your taste buds and get your digestive juices flowing efficiently. It's a delicious breakfast drink, but it would also make a great-tasting non-alcoholic aperitif before a big meal.

Ingredients

1 pink grapefruit, zest and a little pith removed, deseeded and roughly chopped

1 orange zest and a little pith removed, deseeded and roughly chopped

½ lemon, zest and a little pith removed, deseeded and roughly chopped

½ lime, zest and a little pith removed, deseeded and roughly chopped

1–2 lime slices, to decorate

1. Place the grapefruit, orange, lemon and lime in a blender and process until smooth.

2. Pour into glasses and decorate with the lime slices.

Cucumber

Staying hydrated is essential to bodily health and the high water content of cucumber contributes to this. Offering a little something extra than regular water, cucumber contains high levels of vitamin C, vitamin A and an array of anti-oxidants which help to keep your blood pressure down and your skin healthy.

Grapefruit Crush

Serves: 1 | Prep: 10–15 mins | Cook: none

Per serving: 185 KCALS | 1.2G FAT | 0.1G SAT FAT | 43.5G CARBS | 28.7G SUGAR | 3G FIBRE | 4.7G PROTEIN | 0.4G SALT

This fresh and cooling juice is mixed with coconut water, which is packed with electrolytes and minerals to help counter dehydration.

Ingredients

150 g/5½ oz cucumber, roughly chopped

½ pink grapefruit, zest and a little pith removed, deseeded and roughly chopped

2 kiwi fruit, peeled and roughly chopped

2 celery sticks, roughly chopped

1 tsp maca powder

4 tbsp coconut water

1 pink grapefruit segment, to garnish

crushed ice, to serve (optional)

1. Feed the cucumber, grapefruit, kiwi fruit and celery through a juicer.

2. Stir through the maca powder and coconut water until combined.

3. Pour over crushed ice, if using, garnish with a grapefruit segment and serve immediately.

Why not try?

Substitute a flavoured coconut water, such as coconut water with passion fruit or açai.

Dark Beet Thirst-quencher

Serves: 1 | Prep: 10–15 mins| Cook: none

Per serving: 126 KCALS | 1.8G FAT | 0.9G SAT FAT | 26G CARBS | 21.1G SUGAR | 4.8G FIBRE | 4.2G PROTEIN | 0.3G SALT

Cool down on a hot day with this gorgeous-looking thirst-quencher. The natural sweetness of the beetroot will make it surprisingly tempting for kids.

Ingredients

1 orange, deseeded and zest and a little pith removed

85 g/3 oz cooked beetroot

3 tbsp natural yogurt

75 ml/2½ fl oz chilled water

1. Remove a segment from the orange, cut it in half and reserve, then roughly chop the remainder.

2. Put the beetroot and orange in a blender and blend until smooth. Add the yogurt and water and blend again.

3. Pour into a glass. Thread the reserved orange pieces through a cocktail stick, place across the top of the glass and serve.

Stay hydrated

Water makes up about 70 per cent of our muscles and 75 per cent of our brains. In everyday breathing we lose about 500 ml/18 fl oz water, so it is important to keep the body hydrated all year round rather than just when the weather is hot.

Apple Cooler

Serves: 2 | Prep: 15 mins| Cook: none

Per serving: 172 KCALS | 0.7G FAT | TRACE SAT FAT | 42.5G CARBS | 33.5G SUGAR | 3.4G FIBRE | 1.9G PROTEIN | TRACE SALT

This delicious combination of fruits is given added tanginess with the addition of orange juice. Apples and strawberries are both naturally very sweet, so be sure to taste the juice before adding any extra sugar.

Ingredients

2 apples, peeled and roughly chopped
55 g/2 oz strawberries, hulled
juice of 4 oranges
sugar (optional)
4 apple slices, to decorate

1. Put the apples, strawberries and orange juice into a blender and process until smooth.

2. Taste and sweeten with sugar, if using.

3. Decorate with the apple slices and serve immediately.

New to spirulina?

Made from cultivated algae, spirulina contains chlorophyll, vitamin E, the B group of vitamins, linolenic acid, calcium, iron, protein and zinc. Look out for it in packs in health food shops.

Green Steam

Serves: 1 | Prep: 10–15 mins | Cook: none

Per serving: 205 KCALS | 1.4G FAT | 0.2G SAT FAT | 46.5G CARBS | 32.7G SUGAR | 2.1G FIBRE | 6.7G PROTEIN | 0.2G SALT

As melon contains such a high proportion of water, it is great for rehydrating. The addition of spirulina, which contains blood-cleansing chlorophyll, makes this juice perfect for purifying the system.

Ingredients

85 g/3 oz sugar snap peas
5-cm/2-inch piece cucumber
2 kiwi fruit, peeled and roughly chopped
¼ honeydew melon, peeled and thickly sliced
1 tsp spirulina powder (optional)
250 ml/9 fl oz chilled water
small handful of crushed ice (optional)
1 cucumber stick, to serve

1. Feed the peas, cucumber and kiwi fruit through a juicer, followed by the melon slices.

2. Stir in the spirulina powder, if using, and top up with the water.

3. Half-fill a glass with crushed ice, if using, then pour in the juice and serve immediately with a cucumber stick for a stirrer.

For times when you want to up your intake of vitamins, minerals and 'the good stuff', these healthy juices are the easy answer. Recipes like our Vegetable Belly Treat, Spring Clean, Up the Anti and Winter Pick-me-up are sure to help you on your way to feeling nourished and healthy. And the fact that they all taste and look delicious is just a happy bonus!

NOURISH

Crimson Vitality

Serves: 1 | Prep: 10–15 mins | Cook: none

Per serving: 287 KCALS | 0.9G FAT | 0.1G SAT FAT | 74.1G CARBS | 49.5G SUGAR | 3.9G FIBRE | 3G PROTEIN | 0.2G SALT

Good health depends on every cell in the body receiving its fair share of nutrition. Your blood absorbs vital nutrition and circulates round the body. This vitality-boosting juice is an easy way for the body to digest vital vitamins and minerals.

Ingredients

1 beetroot, halved
115 g/4 oz cranberries
1-cm/½-inch piece fresh ginger, peeled
2 apples, quartered
small handful of crushed ice (optional)
chilled water, to taste

1. Feed the beetroot, then the cranberries and ginger, then the apples through a juicer.

2. Half-fill a glass with crushed ice, if using, pour in the juice, top up with water to taste and serve immediately.

Use the beetroot leaves!

If your beetroot has fresh, vibrant leaves rather than tired, limp-looking ones, add them to the juicer too.

Muscular magic
Natural apple booster

Muscular Magic

Serves: 1 | Prep: 15–20 mins | Cook: none

Per serving: 530 KCALS | 32.3G FAT | 3.4G SAT FAT | 59.1G CARBS | 27.8G SUGAR | 13.3G FIBRE | 15.5G PROTEIN | 0.3G SALT

Ingredients

55 g/2 oz green curly kale

small handful of fresh flat-leaf parsley

½ head of cos lettuce

2 celery sticks, halved

1 apple, halved

½ lemon, zest and a little pith removed

30 g/1 oz flaked almonds

½ avocado, stoned, flesh scooped from the skin

small handful of crushed ice

1. Feed the kale, then the parsley and lettuce, then the celery, apple and lemon through a juicer.

2. Put the almonds in a blender and whizz until finely ground. Add the kale juice mix and avocado flesh and blend again until smooth. Add the crushed ice and blend again until smooth.

3. Pour into a glass and serve immediately.

Natural Apple Booster

Serves: 1 | Prep: 10–15 mins| Cook: none

Per serving: 386 KCALS | 10G FAT | 1G SAT FAT | 81.7G CARBS | 62.5G SUGAR | 3.6G FIBRE | 1.4G PROTEIN | TRACE SALT

Ingredients

3 apples, halved

2 tsp flaxseed oil

1 tsp clear honey

¼ tsp ground cinnamon

small handful of crushed ice (optional)

1 cinnamon stick (optional)

1. Feed the apples through a juicer. Stir in the oil, honey and ground cinnamon.

2. Pour the juice into a blender, add the crushed ice, if using, and blend until smooth.

3. Pour into a glass and serve with the cinnamon stick as a stirrer, if using.

Kiwi Juice

Serves: 1 | Prep: 10 mins | Cook: none

Per serving: 216 KCALS | 0.9G FAT | 0.1G SAT FAT | 56G CARBS | 42.9G SUGAR | 7.5G FIBRE | 2.1G PROTEIN | TRACE SALT

Kiwi fruit is loaded with vitamin C, each fruit providing more of this protective vitamin than that traditional source, the orange. Green grapes, apples and kiwi fruit are all high in fibre, so do your digestion a favour with this delicious juice.

Ingredients

1 kiwi fruit, peeled and roughly chopped
1 apple, halved
115 g/4 oz seedless green grapes
crushed ice, to serve (optional)

1. Put the kiwi fruit and apple into a blender and blend until smooth.

2. Add the grapes and process again.

3. Pour into a glass and serve, or pour over crushed ice, if using.

Cranberry & Pineapple Fatigue-buster

Serves: 1 | Prep: 15 mins | Cook: none

Per serving: 324 KCALS | 9.6G FAT | 1G SAT FAT | 59.2G CARBS | 29.5G SUGAR | 17.9G FIBRE | 6.8G PROTEIN | TRACE SALT

This fruit combination works really well, with the natural sweetness of the pineapple balancing the sharpness of the cranberries. Take it to a training session in a flask to give a boost to valuable glycogen stores before and after a workout.

Ingredients

30 g/1 oz chia seeds

½ small pineapple, peeled and roughly chopped

115 g/4 oz cranberries

small handful of crushed ice (optional)

1. Put the chia seeds in a blender and blend until finely ground.

2. Add the pineapple and cranberries and blend until smooth.

3. Half-fill a glass with crushed ice, if using, then pour in the juice and serve immediately.

Soothing pineapple

Rich in energy-boosting fruit sugars and vitamin C, pineapple also contains the digestive enzyme bromelain, which can have a calming effect on the stomach and so help anyone who feels nauseous after a strenuous workout or marathon run.

Vegetable Belly Treat

Serves: 1 | Prep: 15–20 mins | Cook: none

Per serving: 302 KCALS | 10.5G FAT | 1.4G SAT FAT | 50.3G CARBS | 37.1G SUGAR | 8G FIBRE | 5.8G PROTEIN | 0.1G SALT

Wake up your body and stimulate your digestive system with this fresh-tasting orange and tomato drink. The chilli delivers a kick in the tail, so those taste buds will definitely be shaken up!

Ingredients

3 oranges, zest and a little pith removed

1 carrot, halved

2 tomatoes, roughly chopped

125 ml/4 fl oz chilled water

1 small green chilli, halved

2 celery sticks, thickly sliced

2 tsp hempseed oil

1. Cut 2 oranges in half and feed through a juicer with the carrot. Pour the juice into a blender.

2. Roughly chop and deseed the remaining orange, then put it in the blender with the tomatoes and water and blend until smooth. Add the chilli and celery and blend again until smooth.

3. Pour into a glass, stir in the oil and serve.

Hurrah for hempseed oil

Hempseed oil contains a good balance of both omega-3 and omega-6 fats. The Department of Health finds that it is the balance of these fats that is most important in maintaining health and protecting us from disease.

Super Greens

Serves: 1 | Prep: 15–20 mins | Cook: none

Per serving: 323 KCALS | 18.7G FAT | 2.9G SAT FAT | 41.7G CARBS | 20G SUGAR | 10G FIBRE | 5.7G PROTEIN | 0.1G SALT

This super-smoothie is packed with antioxidants, vitamins and minerals. The spirulina is also a great protein-booster.

Ingredients

1 pear, halved

40 g/1½ oz young spinach

4 fresh flat-leaf parsley sprigs

¼ cucumber, roughly chopped

½ avocado, stoned, flesh scooped from the skin

½ tsp spirulina powder

chilled water, to taste

1 Brazil nut, roughly chopped

1. Feed the pear through a juicer. Pour the juice into a blender, add the spinach, parsley, cucumber and avocado and blend until smooth. Pour into a glass.

2. Mix the spirulina with just enough water to make a thick liquid, then swirl this into the juice.

3. Sprinkle over the chopped Brazil nut and serve.

Apricot Buzz

Serves: 2 | Prep 10–15 mins | Cook: none

Per serving: 86 KCALS | 0.5G FAT | TRACE SAT FAT | 20.4G CARBS | 15.8G SUGAR | 4.2G FIBRE | 2.1G PROTEIN | TRACE SALT

When apricots are ripe and bursting with flavour, this nutritious juice will really go down well. Serve with ice on a warm summer morning.

Ingredients

6 apricots, stoned

1 orange, zest and a little pith removed, deseeded and roughly chopped

1 fresh lemon grass stalk, roughly chopped

2-cm/¾-inch piece fresh ginger, peeled

ice cubes, to serve

1. Place the apricots, orange, lemon grass and ginger in a blender and blend until combined.

2. Pour the mixture into glasses, add ice and serve.

Cinnamon

Cinnamon contains anti-inflammatory properties and it also has the ability to stabilise blood sugar levels, a function of particular interest to diabetes sufferers. Its spiciness has a curative impact on the common cold and respiratory infections, and its warming quality almost makes the internal nourishment it provides something tangible.

Say yes to soya!

Adding soya yogurt or soya milk to a juice is a great way to boost its protein levels. Choose soya yogurt or milk that is unsweetened.

Cherry Pink

Serves: 1 | Prep: 20–25 mins | Cook: none

Per serving: 389 KCALS | 1.8G FAT | 0.2G SAT FAT | 98.6G CARBS | 75.6G SUGAR | 12.7G FIBRE | 5.7G PROTEIN | TRACE SALT

This creamy drink is made with soya yogurt which boosts its calcium content and is suitable for vegans and vegetarians. Delicious grapes and cherries provide an antioxidant boost, and the sweet flavours are rounded out with the tang of lime.

Ingredients

350 g/12 oz dark sweet cherries, stoned

1 apple, halved

½ lime, zest and pith removed, deseeded and roughly chopped

100 g/3½ oz red grapes

40 g/1½ oz soya yogurt

1. Put the cherries, apple, lime and grapes into a blender and blend until smooth. Whisk in the yogurt.

2. Pour into a glass and serve.

Spring clean
Body balance

Spring Clean

Serves: 1 | Prep: 15 mins | Cook: none

Per serving : 259 KCALS | 1.3G FAT | 0.2G SAT FAT | 63G CARBS | 42.2G SUGAR | 4.9G FIBRE | 6.3G PROTEIN | 0.1G SALT

Ingredients

115 g/4 oz broccoli, broken into large florets

2 apples, halved

1 courgette, halved

1 tsp wheatgrass powder

small handful of crushed ice

1. Feed the broccoli, then the apples and courgette through a juicer.

2. Add the wheatgrass powder to the juice and whisk until smooth.

3. Half-fill a glass with crushed ice, pour in the juice and serve immediately.

Body Balance

Serves: 1 | Prep: 15 mins | Cook: none

Per serving : 576 KCALS | 8.3G FAT | 0.8G SAT FAT | 123.3G CARBS | 73.9G SUGAR | 13.8G FIBRE | 11.9G PROTEIN | TRACE SALT

Ingredients

1 tbsp linseeds

85 g/3 oz ready-to-eat stoned prunes

1 small banana, peeled and roughly chopped

1 tbsp wheat germ

juice of 2 large oranges

125 ml/4 fl oz vanilla soya yogurt

225 ml/8 fl oz chilled water

1. Put the linseeds into a blender and whizz until finely ground. Add the prunes, banana and wheat germ and blend until smooth.

2. Add the orange juice and half the yogurt and blend again until smooth. Add the water and blend once more.

3. Pour into a glass, add the remaining yogurt and swirl together with a teaspoon, then serve.

Good-for-you ginger

Ginger has been used as a natural remedy for centuries, especially for ailments involving the digestive system. Pregnant women are often encouraged to drink ginger tea to prevent morning sickness. Recent studies have shown that ginger may also help with menstrual cramps, migraines, colds, flu and heartburn.

Ginger Energizer

Serves: 1 | Prep: 15 mins | Cook: none

Per serving: 134 KCALS | 1.2G FAT | TRACE SAT FAT | 29.7G CARBS | 16.2G SUGAR | 6.3G FIBRE | 5.4G PROTEIN | 0.2G SALT

The ginger in this oh-so-good-for-you vegetable drink will pep you up when you're feeling a bit tired and your system is sluggish.

Ingredients

2 carrots, halved

4 tomatoes, roughly chopped

1 tbsp lemon juice

30 g/1 oz fresh flat-leaf parsley

3-cm/1¼-inch piece fresh ginger, peeled and finely grated

small handful of crushed ice

125 ml/4 fl oz chilled water

1. Feed the carrots through a juicer. Pour the juice into a blender, add the tomatoes and lemon juice and blend.

2. Add the parsley (reserving a sprig to decorate), ginger and crushed ice and blend again until smooth. Add the water and whizz again.

3. Pour into a glass, garnish with the parsley sprig and serve immediately.

Up the Anti

Serves: 1 | Prep: 15–20 mins, plus chilling | Cook: none

Per serving: 250 KCALS | 15G FAT | 3.5G SAT FAT | 18G CARBS | 18G SUGAR | 6G FIBRE | 3G PROTEIN | TRACE SALT

Protect your body from the inside out with this fresh, fruity drink that is bursting with antioxidants, the body's natural defence team.

Ingredients

½ avocado, stoned, flesh scooped from the skin
115 g/4 oz blueberries
115 g/4 oz strawberries, hulled
juice of 1 tangerine or small orange
125 ml/4 fl oz chilled water
small handful of crushed ice (optional)

1. Put the avocado, blueberries, strawberries, tangerine juice and water into a blender and blend to combine.

2. Add the crushed ice, if using, and blend again until smooth.

3. Pour into a glass and serve immediately.

Avocado benefits

Avocados may inhibit the growth of prostate cancer and, being high in oleic acid, they may also help to prevent breast cancer. They contain more of the carotenoid lutein than any other commonly consumed fruit. Lutein protects against macular degeneration and cataracts, two disabling age-related eye diseases. Eating avocados may also lower your cholesterol levels and, as an excellent source of glutathione, they even contain anti-ageing properties.

Pear & Raspberry Delight

Serves: 2 | Prep: 15 mins | Cook: none

Per serving: 331 KCALS | 1.5G FAT | 0.1G SAT FAT | 86G CARBS | 50.7G SUGAR | 15.9G FIBRE | 3.3G PROTEIN | TRACE SALT

Frozen fruit and vegetables are extremely useful to have on standby, and are just as nutritionally sound as the fresh versions – sometimes more so, as they are usually frozen very soon after harvesting, locking in the maximum goodness.

Ingredients

2 large ripe Conference pears, halved
125 g/4½ oz frozen raspberries
200 ml/7 fl oz ice-cold water
honey (optional)
4 raspberries, to decorate

1. Put the pears into a blender with the raspberries and water and blend until smooth.

2. Taste and sweeten with honey, if using, if the raspberries are a little too sharp for your taste.

3. Pour into glasses, decorate with whole raspberries threaded onto cocktail sticks and serve immediately.

Winter Pick-me-up

Serves: 1 | Prep: 10–15 mins | Cook: none

Per serving: 491 KCALS | 3.5G FAT | 0.6G SAT FAT | 115.7G CARBS | 61.4G SUGAR | 7.8G FIBRE | 8.7G PROTEIN | 0.2G SALT

Banish the winter blues with this nutrient-packed juice that contains essential vitamins and minerals and will boost your energy levels.

Ingredients

1 parsnip, halved
2 carrots, halved
1 garlic clove
2 apples, halved
2 tbsp porridge oats
1 tbsp wheat germ
2 tsp clear honey
small handful of crushed ice (optional)
2 carrot sticks, to garnish

1. Feed the parsnip, carrots and garlic through a juicer, then feed the apples through.

2. Put the oats and wheat germ into a blender and blend until finely ground. Add the honey and parsnip mixture and blend again until smooth.

3. Half-fill a glass with crushed ice, if using. Pour in the juice, garnish with the carrot sticks and serve immediately.

Buying parsnips

Buy parsnips a few weeks after the first frost if you can, because much of the starch is converted to sugar in a frost, making them taste sweeter.

Pomegranate

As one of the most popular fruits championed for its taste, the pomegranate is also packed with nutrients, offering many positive health benefits that nourish the body. It is proven to lower cholesterol and contains a high level of vitamin C, helping the body develop a strong resistance to infectious bacteria and illnesses. Along with this, its natural sweetness boosts energy and it is also said to relieve stress.

Passionate Juice Fizz

Serves: 1 | Prep: 20 mins | Cook: none

Per serving: 327 KCALS | 3.9G FAT | 0.3G SAT FAT | 75.1G CARBS | 51.1G SUGAR | 20G FIBRE | 6.7G PROTEIN | TRACE SALT

This exotic-tasting juice makes good use of passion fruit and pomegranate, whose seeds are embedded in the pulp and are meant to be eaten. Both fruits have delicious flavours that add pep to this sparkling juice.

Ingredients

1 pomegranate, seeds only

½ small orange, zest and pith removed, deseeded and roughly chopped

4 passion fruit, seeds scooped out

100–125 ml/3½–4 fl oz sparkling mineral water

1. Put the pomegranate seeds into a blender, add the orange and three quarters of the passion fruit seeds, then blend until smooth.

2. Pour into a glass and stir in the remaining passion fruit seeds.

3. Top up with the mineral water and serve.

Power-boosting Beet

Serves: 1 | Prep: 10–15 minutes | Cook: none

Per serving: 570 KCALS | 21.1G FAT | 0.9G SAT FAT | 96.1G CARBS | 63.5G SUGAR | 8.3G FIBRE | 11.2G PROTEIN | 1G SALT

With sweet beetroot, carrot and apple, you won't need to add any extra sugar to this energizing drink. The walnuts add depth and texture to this vibrant juice.

Ingredients

2 beetroots, halved
2 large carrots, halved
2 celery sticks, halved
5-cm/2-inch piece cucumber
2 red-skinned apples, halved
30 g/1 oz walnut pieces, finely ground
small handful of crushed ice (optional)

1. Cut two wafer-thin slices off one of the beetroot halves and reserve.

2. Feed the beetroots and carrots, then the celery and cucumber, then the apples through a juicer. Stir in the walnuts. Half-fill a glass with crushed ice, if using, then pour in the juice.

3. Thread the beetroot slices through a cocktail stick, lay this on top of the glass and serve immediately.

Plums for vitamin C

Plums are a great source of vitamin C, which helps you to fight infection and increase iron absorption. But don't eat too many at once, because they are also known to have a laxative effect.

Apple & Plum Power Boost

Serves: 2 | Prep: 15 mins | Cook: 15 mins, plus chilling

Per serving: 148 KCALS | 0.4G FAT | TRACE SAT FAT | 38.2G CARBS | 29.3G SUGAR | 5.8G FIBRE | 1G PROTEIN | TRACE SALT

Cooking the fruit brings out the sweetness and adds a depth of flavour to this smoothie that makes it seem very substantial. For a quick and delicious vitamin boost, you could have it instead of your usual packed lunch.

Ingredients

1 ripe pear, peeled and quartered
1 apple, peeled and quartered
2 large red or dark plums, halved and stoned
4 ripe damsons, halved and stoned
200 ml/7 fl oz water
slices of apple or pear, to decorate

1. Put the pear, apple, plums, damsons and water into a small saucepan. Cover tightly, set over a medium heat and bring slowly to the boil. Remove from the heat and leave to cool. Chill.

2. Put the fruit and water into a food processor or blender and process until smooth.

3. Pour into glasses, decorate with slices of apple or pear and serve.

Lychee & Pineapple Pep-up

Serves: 1 | Prep: 20 mins, plus cooling | Cook: none

Per serving: 280 KCALS | 0.6G FAT | 0.2G SAT FAT | 70.7G CARBS | 57.9G SUGAR | 7G FIBRE | 3.7G PROTEIN | 0.1G SALT

Create a drink with the exotic flavours of South-East Asia, using fragrant lemon grass and lychees blended with pineapple and melon.

Ingredients

1½ lemon grass stalk

4 tbsp boiling water

6 lychees, peeled and stoned

½ small pineapple, peeled and cut into thick slices

¼ honeydew melon, thickly sliced and peeled

small handful of crushed ice (optional)

1. Cut the whole lemon grass stem in half lengthways, then crossways. Bruise it with a rolling pin to release its flavour, then put it in a shallow bowl and add the boiling water. Cover and leave to cool completely, then drain, reserving the soaking water.

2. Feed the softened lemon grass, lychees and pineapple, then the melon through a juicer. Mix in the reserved soaking water.

3. Half-fill a glass with crushed ice, if using, then pour in the juice and serve immediately with the remaining lemon grass as a stirrer.

We all want to look and feel the very best that we can and get that must-have 'glow', but how can we do this in an easy way? It's simple – choose juices and smoothies that are packed with lots of vitamin C, calcium and antioxidants. We've got tons of great choices in this chapter, like Kale Coco Bomb, Berry Booster and Green Colada to help you shine.

GLOW

Skin-soother Smoothie

Serves: 1 | Prep: 10 mins | Cook: none

Per serving: 466 KCALS | 13.4G FAT | 2.1G SAT FAT | 87.5G CARBS | 51.1G SUGAR | 15.7G FIBRE | 10.1G PROTEIN | TRACE SALT

Packed with healing vitamin C from the fruit, skin-protecting vitamin E from the peanut butter and essential fatty acids (EFAs) from the linseeds, this spectacular stripy drink might just be your skin's new best friend.

Ingredients

Banana layer

1 banana, peeled and roughly chopped
1 tbsp smooth peanut butter
1 tbsp soya yogurt

Blueberry layer

150 g/5½ oz blueberries
juice of ½ lemon

Kiwi layer

3 kiwi fruit, peeled and roughly chopped
1 tbsp ground linseeds

1. Put all the ingredients for the banana layer in a blender and blend until smooth. Transfer to a jug and rinse the blender goblet.

2. To make the blueberry layer, put the blueberries and lemon juice into the blender and blend until smooth. Transfer to a separate jug and rinse the blender goblet.

3. To make the kiwi layer, place the kiwi in the blender with the linseeds and blend until smooth. Layer the three smoothie mixtures into a large glass and serve immediately.

Why not try?

Coconut yogurt would work well here, but substitute the yogurt with a splash of cold water if necessary.

Thai Sunrise
Hail the kale

Thai Sunrise

Serves: 1 | Prep: 10–15 mins | Cook: none

Per serving: 148 KCALS | 0.6G FAT | TRACE SAT FAT | 38G CARBS | 23.8G SUGAR | 7.4G FIBRE | 2.6G PROTEIN | 0.1G SALT

Ingredients

50 g/1¾ oz spinach
6 fresh Thai basil leaves
200 ml/7 fl oz chilled water
1 pear, halved
4 fresh lychees, peeled and stoned
5 g/⅛ oz fresh ginger, peeled
juice of ½ lime
1 Thai basil sprig, to garnish

1. Put the spinach, basil and water into a blender and blend until smooth.

2. Add the pear, lychees, ginger and lime juice, and blend until smooth. Serve immediately, garnished with a Thai basil sprig.

Hail the Kale

Serves: 1 | Prep: 10–15 mins| Cook: none

Per serving: 100 KCALS | 10.0G FAT | 1.0G SAT FAT | 10.0G CARBS | 5.0G SUGAR | 1.0G FIBRE | 1.0G PROTEIN | TRACE SALT

Ingredients

30 g/1 oz green curly kale, shredded
50 g/1¾ oz coconut flesh
350 ml/12 fl oz chilled almond milk
1 tbsp sunflower seeds
¼ tsp ground cinnamon
¼ tsp ground cinnamon, to garnish

1. Put the kale in a blender.

2. Add the coconut, almond milk, sunflower seeds and cinnamon, and blend until smooth and creamy (this might take a little longer than usual due to the coconut).

3. Serve immediately, sprinkled with cinnamon.

Kiwi Quencher

Serves: 1 | Prep: 15 mins | Cook: none

Per serving: 414 KCALS | 2.5G FAT | 0.2G SAT FAT | 103.5G CARBS | 67.5G SUGAR | 20.6G FIBRE | 7.3G PROTEIN | TRACE SALT

What a combo: cool, jewel-like kiwi fruit blended with naturally juicy green grapes and thirst-quenching crisp, fresh lettuce.

Ingredients

½ head of cos lettuce
4 kiwi fruit, peeled
115 g/4 oz green grapes
1 large pear, halved
small handful of crushed ice, to serve (optional)

1. Peel off a lettuce leaf and reserve.

2. Feed the kiwi fruit and grapes, then the lettuce and pear through a juicer.

3. Half-fill a glass with crushed ice, if using, then pour in the juice. Decorate with the reserved lettuce leaf and serve immediately.

Ruby Fruit Reviver

Serves: 1 | Prep: 15–20 mins | Cook: none

Per serving: 162 KCALS | 0.8G FAT | TRACE SAT FAT | 40.4G CARBS | 25.5G SUGAR | 7.3G FIBRE | 3.4G PROTEIN | TRACE SALT

There's nothing more refreshing than a locally grown strawberry in season, so this smoothie is best enjoyed in the early summer – shop carefully for strawberries that really smell and taste as they should: biggest doesn't necessarily mean best!

Ingredients

1 ruby red grapefruit, zest and a little pith removed, deseeded and roughly chopped

¼ cucumber, roughly chopped

150 g/5½ oz strawberries, hulled

small handful of crushed ice (optional)

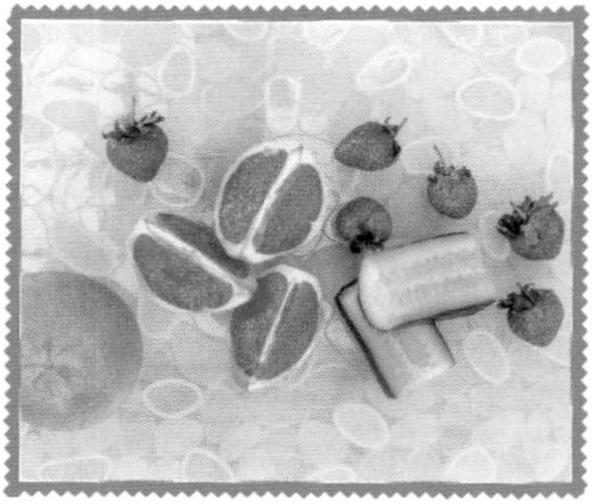

1. Put the grapefruit and cucumber in a blender and blend until smooth.

2. Add the strawberries and crushed ice, if using, and blend again until smooth and combined.

3. Pour into a glass and serve immediately.

Freezing bananas

To freeze bananas, peel them, then freeze them on a tray for 30 minutes, spaced well apart. When frozen, transfer to polythene bags or plastic containers. Use within 3–4 months.

Kale Coco Bomb

Serves: 1 | Prep: 10–15 mins | Cook: none

Per serving: 133 KCALS | 2.4G FAT | 0.4G SAT FAT | 28.1G CARBS | 13.1G SUGAR | 5.1G FIBRE | 4.3G PROTEIN | TRACE SALT

This creamy smoothie tastes like a naughty treat but with nutrient-rich kale and raw cacao powder it is actually very good for you! It also makes good use of those frozen bananas in your freezer.

Ingredients

40 g/1½ oz green curly kale, shredded

200 ml/7 fl oz chilled water

1 tsp hemp seeds or hempseed oil

100 g/3½ oz frozen banana

1 tsp raw cacao powder

¼ vanilla pod, seeds scraped

small pinch of raw cacao powder, to garnish

1. Put the kale in a blender with the water, and blend until smooth.

2. Add the hemp seeds, banana, cacao powder and vanilla seeds and blend again until smooth and creamy.

3. Pour into a glass and serve immediately, garnished with a pinch of raw cacao.

Super-powered Mango

Serves: 1 | Prep: 15–20 mins | Cook: none

Per serving: 460 KCALS | 2G FAT | 0.3G SAT FAT | 118.9G CARBS | 98.2G SUGAR | 4G FIBRE | 4.6G PROTEIN | TRACE SALT

The mango gives a simply delicious tropical flavour to this refreshing juice. If you can't get clementines, use mandarin oranges instead, but be sure to deseed them. You may need to add an extra teaspoon of honey, as clementines are sweeter.

Ingredients

2 clementines, zest and a little pith removed

1 mango, stoned and peeled

2 apples, halved

small handful of crushed ice, to serve (optional)

chilled water, to taste

1 tsp clear honey

1. Feed the clementines, mango and apples through a juicer.

2. Half-fill a glass with crushed ice, if using. Pour in the juice, top up with water to taste, stir in the honey and serve immediately.

Minted Melon Drink

Serves: 1 | Prep: 15 mins | Cook: none

Per serving: 153 KCALS | 0.6G FAT | 0.2G SAT FAT | 38.8G CARBS | 32.7G SUGAR | 0.9G FIBRE | 2.6G PROTEIN | 0.2G SALT

Did you ever think that it was a waste to throw away the broccoli stem and half the weight of the vegetable? The stem has just as many nutrients as the florets, yet it is often binned, although it is a valuable addition to soups and juices.

Ingredients

½ honeydew melon, thickly sliced and peeled

5 fresh mint sprigs

½ lime, zest and a little pith removed

2.5-cm/1-inch slice of broccoli stem

small handful of crushed ice (optional)

1. Feed the melon and mint, then the lime and broccoli through a juicer.

2. Half-fill a glass with crushed ice, if using, then pour in the juice and serve immediately.

Give green juice a chance

Green juicing is no longer the preserve of movie stars, supermodels and vegans. Everyone's gone mad for it, and no wonder. If you want to look after your health, well-being, weight and appearance, there is surely no easier way to do it than by incorporating juicing into your diet. Always buy the best-quality, freshest products you can find – they contain more nutrients and flavour. Avoid anything discoloured or wilted, which will have lost vitamins B and C and enzymes.

Berry Booster

Serves: 1 | Prep: 15 mins| Cook: none

Per serving: 129 KCALS | 1.3G FAT | TRACE SAT FAT | 29.8G CARBS | 15.2G SUGAR | 13G FIBRE | 3.2G PROTEIN | TRACE SALT

Think of this juice as the ultimate beauty treatment: it will rehydrate your skin and plump up and reduce those wrinkles, and the vitamin C-loaded berries will help clear up those annoying spots and blemishes.

Ingredients

150 g/5½ oz strawberries
85 g/3 oz raspberries
85 g/3 oz blackberries
175 ml/6 fl oz chilled water
small handful of crushed ice (optional)

1. Cut a strawberry in half and reserve one half, along with a raspberry and a blackberry. Hull the remaining strawberries.

2. Put the strawberries, raspberries, blackberries and water in a blender and blend until smooth. Half-fill a glass with crushed ice, if using, then pour in the berry juice.

3. Thread the reserved fruit onto a wooden skewer to make a stirrer, then serve with the juice.

Berry bonus

We all know that summer berries contain vitamin C, but did you know that raspberries contain manganese, which helps with the metabolism of carbohydrates, proteins and cholesterol and helps to keep our bones healthy?

Broccoli

Around 75 g/2½oz of broccoli contains 135% of the daily amount of vitamin C the body needs, offering anti-blemish and anti-wrinkles for the skin, providing a soothed complexion and a healthy glow. Broccoli also contains a large amount of the nutrient carotene which offers anti-oxidant protection, helping to maintain the skin's glow, whilst protecting and cleansing the body in general.

Boost it!

To make this delicious juice even more nutritious, add 1 teaspoon of spirulina for a calcium hit.

Beet It!

Serves: 1 | Prep: 10–15 mins | Cook: none

Per serving: 191 KCALS | 1.2G FAT | 0.1G SAT FAT | 44.6G CARBS | 27.6G SUGAR | 2.6G FIBRE | 6.1G PROTEIN | 0.5G SALT

Earthy and sweet beetroot brings a lot to the table. The leaves should not be discarded either – they can be enjoyed in the same way as spinach.

Ingredients

40 g/1½ oz rocket
150 g/5½ oz radicchio
40 g/1½ oz beetroot leaves
1 green apple, halved
1 beetroot, halved

1. Feed the rocket, radicchio, beetroot leaves, apple and beetroot through a juicer.

2. Stir well, pour into a glass and serve immediately.

Green Apple & Kiwi Juice

Serves: 2 | Prep: 10–15 mins | Cook: none

Per serving: 160 KCALS | 0.8G FAT | 0.1G SAT FAT | 41.5G CARBS | 27.3G SUGAR | 21.5G FIBRE | 2.2G PROTEIN | TRACE SALT

Apples are rich in vitamin C, which is great for maintaining the elasticity of your skin and keeping your hair healthy and shiny. The addition of cucumber will benefit your skin, helping to keep it clear and free of blemishes.

Ingredients

2 green apples, such as Granny Smith, halved

½ cucumber, roughly chopped

2 kiwi fruit, peeled and roughly chopped

½ lemon, zest and pith removed, seeded and roughly chopped

2-cm/¾-inch piece fresh ginger, peeled and roughly chopped

1. Feed all of the ingredients through a juicer.

2. Transfer the juice to tall glasses and serve immediately.

Blackberry Blaster

Serves: 1 | Prep: 15 mins | Cook: none

Per serving: 333 KCALS | 3.6G FAT | 0.3G SAT FAT | 74.6G CARBS | 43.5G SUGAR | 6.5G FIBRE | 9.9G PROTEIN | TRACE SALT

Banish those morning blues with this cinnamon-spiced dairy-free juice. It's bursting with vitamins and minerals, and will keep you energized until lunchtime.

Ingredients

3 large red-skinned plums, halved and stoned

40 g/1½ oz red curly kale

1 pear, halved

115 g/4 oz blackberries

20 g/¾ oz wheat germ

¼ tsp ground cinnamon (optional)

small handful of crushed ice

4–6 tbsp chilled water

1. Feed the plums, then the kale, then the pear through a juicer. Pour the juice into a blender. Add the blackberries (reserving one to decorate), wheat germ, cinnamon, if using, and crushed ice and blend until smooth.

2. Add the water to taste and blend again until smooth. Pour into a glass.

3. Thread a blackberry through a cocktail stick, add it to the glass and serve immediately.

Blackberries: nature's aspirin

Energy-boosting blackberries are a good source of vitamin C, folates and fibre. More unusually, they also contain salicylates, a natural aspirin-like compound, so if you are allergic to aspirin steer clear of this fruit.

Boost it!

Boost this juice's nutritional power and get your skin glowing by adding 2 teaspoons of acai powder.

Sprout Tonic

Serves: 1 | Prep: 10–15 mins | Cook: none

Per serving: 162 KCALS | 2.7G FAT | 0G SAT FAT | 31.8G CARBS | 15.2G SUGAR | 5G FIBRE | 4.2G PROTEIN | 0.5G SALT

Brussels sprouts might seem like a Christmas dinner staple, but drinking them in a smoothie like this means you can eat your greens all year round.

Ingredients

75 g/2¾ oz Brussels sprouts
30 g/1 oz beetroot leaves
30 g/1 oz chard
250 ml/9 fl oz unsweetened rice milk

1. Put the Brussels sprouts, beetroot leaves and chard into a blender.

2. Pour over the rice milk and blend until smooth and creamy.

3. Pour into a glass and serve immediately.

Kiwi

Kiwi fruit is full of omega-3, important in preventing an array of skin diseases and protecting the health of cell membranes. As a strong provider of vitamin C and vitamin E, it helps to maintain the skin's moisture and aids the healing of cuts and scars.

Mango & Lime Bone-builder

Serves: 1 | Prep: 15 mins | Cook: none

Per serving: 346 KCALS | 10G FAT | 1.7G SAT FAT | 57.6G CARBS | 46.4G SUGAR | 8.5G FIBRE | 11G PROTEIN | 0.1G SALT

The natural sweetness of mango perfectly balances the kale in this pretty, green-speckled drink, which will boost your calcium intake, ensuring strong bones.

Ingredients

1 tbsp sesame seeds

juice of ½ lime

30 g/1 oz green curly kale, shredded

1 mango, peeled, stoned and roughly chopped

225 ml/8 fl oz unsweetened rice, almond or soya milk

small handful of crushed ice

1. Put the sesame seeds into a blender and whizz until finely ground.

2. Add the lime juice, kale and mango and blend until well combined.

3. Add the milk and crushed ice and blend again until smooth. Pour into a glass and serve immediately.

Good for your bones

The calcium-boosting sesame seeds and kale help to maintain bone strength and muscle function.

Did you know?

Coconut milk comes in two varieties – thick and thin. The thinner milk, available in a carton, has a much lower fat content than the thicker milk that comes in a tin. The thinner milk is ideal for juices and smoothies or just as a replacement for dairy milk.

Green Colada

Serves: 1 | Prep: 10–15 mins | Cook: none

Per serving: 115 KCALS | 5.4G FAT | 4G SAT FAT | 14.5G CARBS | 5.3G SUGAR | 1.7G FIBRE | 4.9G PROTEIN | 0.4G SALT

This elegant and deliciously refreshing drink is an excellent calcium booster and provides the vitamins and minerals needed for a healthy and glowing complexion.

Ingredients

100 g/3½ oz spinach, roughly chopped
100 g/3½ oz cucumber, roughly chopped
20 g/¾ oz fresh mint
200 ml/7 fl oz coconut milk
½ tsp linseeds
1 tsp chlorophyll powder
1 fresh mint sprig, to garnish
crushed ice, to serve

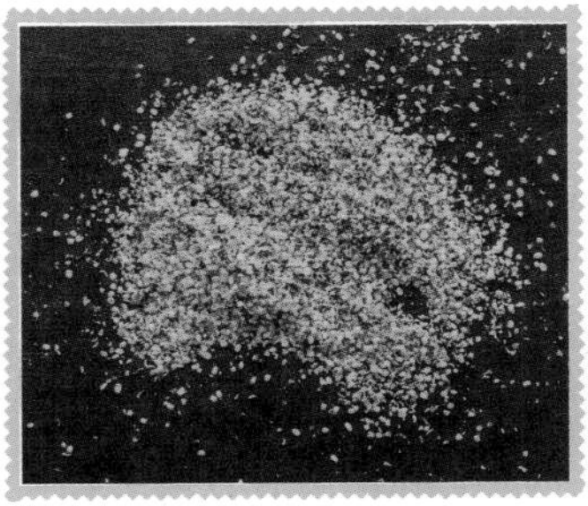

1. Feed the spinach and cucumber through a juicer with the mint.

2. Stir through the coconut milk, linseeds and chlorophyll powder until thoroughly combined.

3. Fill a glass with crushed ice, pour in the juice, garnish with a mint sprig and serve immediately.

Fresh & Fruity

Serves: 1 | Prep: 10–15 mins | Cook: none

Per serving: 219 KCALS | 1.1G FAT | TRACE SAT FAT | 55.3G CARBS | 38.9G SUGAR | 10.2G FIBRE | 3.1G PROTEIN | TRACE SALT

The pineapple in this smoothie will help prevent constipation, promoting a clear complexion, and the blackberries and blueberries are high in the antioxidants that combat the free radicals known to damage the skin's youthful elasticity.

Ingredients

½ small pineapple, peeled and roughly chopped

85 g/3 oz blackberries

85 g/3 oz blueberries

1 tsp goji berries, roughly chopped, to decorate

1. Put the pineapple in a blender with the blackberries and blueberries and blend until smooth.

2. Pour into a glass, sprinkle with the chopped goji berries and serve.

Cranberry Soother

Serves: 1 | Prep: 10 mins | Cook: none

Per serving: 205 KCALS | 3.2G FAT | 1.9G SAT FAT | 42.7G CARBS | 29.4G SUGAR | 5.6G FIBRE | 4.4G PROTEIN | 0.1G SALT

Help to protect your body with this wonderfully colourful and tasty drink. It's a great way to encourage your children to eat more vitamin C-packed fruit, too.

Ingredients

150 g/5½ oz cranberries
juice of 1 orange
5 tbsp natural yogurt
2 tsp clear honey

1. Put the cranberries and orange juice into a blender and blend until smooth.

2. Add the yogurt and honey and blend again.

3. Pour into a glass and serve immediately.

Grape Nutrient-booster

Serves: 1 | Prep: 15 mins | Cook: none

Per serving: 416 KCALS | 5.7G FAT | 0.9G SAT FAT | 94.5G CARBS | 62.6G SUGAR | 6.3G FIBRE | 9.3G PROTEIN | 0.1G SALT

Naturally sweet pears and grapes are a terrific way to disguise the taste of nutritious vegetables such as cabbage in a juice. As the pumpkin seeds in this drink are finely ground, no one will know they are there either!

Ingredients

2 pears, halved

¼ small head of Savoy cabbage, roughly chopped

1 tbsp pumpkin seeds

150 g/5½ oz seedless green grapes

small handful of crushed ice (optional)

1. Feed the pears and cabbage through a juicer.

2. Put the pumpkin seeds into a blender and whizz until finely ground, then add the grapes and crushed ice, if using, and blend. Pour in the pear juice mix and blend until smooth.

3. Pour into a glass and serve immediately.

Cabbage nutrition

Savoy cabbage is a storehouse of phytochemicals and powerful antioxidants, which are thought to help protect against cancer. It also contains a huge range of vitamins and minerals, not to mention beta-carotene and the amino acid glutamine (an anti-inflammatory).

Making a delicious smoothie when you have digestive problems can have huge benefits. Not only can it help relax, comfort and soothe you as you drink but it can have a range of real health benefits for your digestive tract. This chapter is full of ideal choices like Mellow Mr Green, Cucumber Soother and Broccoli Booster that are kind on your stomach but full of flavour.

SOOTHE

Melon & Coconut Mojito

Serves: 1 | Prep: 10–15 mins | Cook: none

Per serving: 265 KCALS | 17.3G FAT | 14.9G SAT FAT | 28.8G CARBS | 21G SUGAR | 7.4G FIBRE | 4G PROTEIN | TRACE SALT

This fresh and fruity smoothie will bring back happy memories of hot summer days. With cooling mint and melon and refreshing tropical coconut and mango, it will be hard to beat as a hot weather soother.

Ingredients

20 g/¾ oz spinach

50 g/1¾ oz coconut flesh

200 ml/7 fl oz chilled water

100 g/3½ oz cantaloupe melon, peeled and deseeded

1 tbsp chopped fresh mint

juice of ½ lime

50 g/1¾ oz mango, stoned and peeled

1 mango slice, stoned and peeled, to garnish

crushed ice, to serve

1. Put the spinach, coconut and water into a blender and blend until smooth.

2. Add the melon, mint, lime juice and mango and blend again until smooth and creamy.

3. Pour over crushed ice, if using, and serve immediately, garnished with the mango slice.

Greek Green
Mellow Mr Green

Greek Green

Serves: 1 | Prep: 10–15 mins | Cook: none

Per serving: 308 KCALS | 24G FAT | 13.2G SAT FAT | 12.8G CARBS | 6.7G SUGAR | 4.8G FIBRE | 13.9G PROTEIN | 0.1G SALT

Ingredients

15 g/½ oz curly green kale, shredded

200 ml/7 fl oz chilled water

¼ vanilla pod, seeds scraped

100 g/3½ oz Greek-style yogurt

30 g/1 oz coconut flesh

1 tbsp almond butter

1. Put the kale in a blender with the water and blend until smooth and creamy.

2. Add the vanilla seeds to the blender with the yogurt, coconut and almond butter, and blend until smooth. Serve immediately.

Mellow Mr Green

Serves: 1 | Prep: 15 mins | Cook: none

Per serving: 306 KCALS | 21.8G FAT | 15G SAT FAT | 28.1G CARBS | 19.3G SUGAR | 5.2G FIBRE | 6.3G PROTEIN | 0.1G SALT

Ingredients

10 g/¼ oz rocket

200 ml/7 fl oz chilled water

1 kiwi fruit, peeled and roughly chopped

150 g/5½ oz canteloupe melon, peeled, deseeded and roughly chopped

3 tbsp coconut cream

2 tsp smooth peanut butter

1. Put the rocket and water into a blender and blend until smooth.

2. Add the kiwi fruit and melon to the blender with the coconut cream and peanut butter and blend until creamy. Serve immediately.

Bee Pollen & Nectarine Soother

Serves: 2 | Prep: 15 mins | Cook: none

Per serving: 163 KCALS | 3.2G FAT | 1.8G SAT FAT | 28.7G CARBS | 22.8G SUGAR | 2.6G FIBRE | 7.3G PROTEIN | 0.1G SALT

Nutritious bee pollen adds an intriguing touch to this nifty and nourishing nectarine milkshake. Milk and natural yogurt team up to create a calcium-rich base, and the honey adds a touch of natural sweetness.

Ingredients

2 ripe nectarines, stoned and quartered
200 ml/7 fl oz semi-skimmed milk
2 tbsp Greek-style natural yogurt
1 tbsp bee pollen
1 tsp clear honey
handful of ice cubes
1 tsp bee pollen, to decorate
2 slices nectarine, to decorate

1. Place the nectarines, milk, yogurt, bee pollen and honey in a blender and blend until smooth. Add the ice cubes and blend again until completely blended.

2. Pour the milkshake into chilled glasses and decorate each with the bee pollen and a slice of nectarine. Serve immediately.

Why not try?

If you like your smoothies a little sweeter, add some more honey to the recipe.

Super Smoothie

Serves: 1 | Prep: 10–15 mins | Cook: none

Per serving: 308 KCALS | 17.2G FAT | 2.4G SAT FAT | 40.3G CARBS | 15.2G SUGAR | 12.7G FIBRE | 5.3G PROTEIN | 0.1G SALT

The avocado is a nutrient-dense food that helps the body to absorb fat-soluble nutrients. If that isn't enough to persuade you to add avocados to smoothies, do it because it makes them creamy and soothing!

Ingredients

30 g/1 oz spinach

250 ml/9 fl oz cooled liquorice tea

½ avocado, stoned, flesh scooped from the skin

1 frozen banana

1 tsp chia seeds

½ tsp chia seeds, to garnish

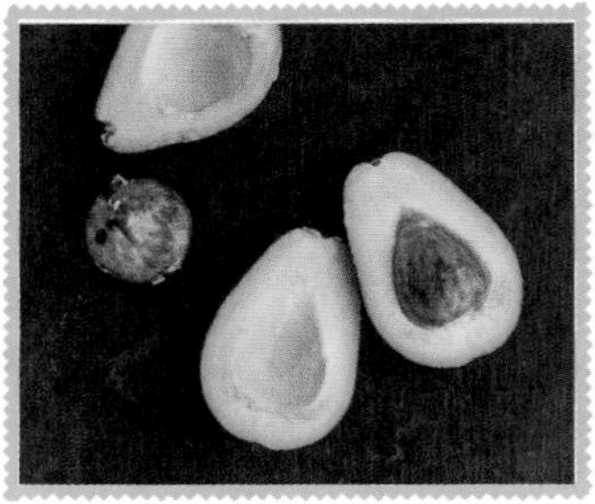

1. Put the spinach and liquorice tea into a blender and blend until smooth.

2. Chop the avocado, add it to the blender with the banana and chia seeds and blend until smooth and creamy.

3. Serve immediately, garnished with a sprinkling of chia seeds.

Freezing fruit

When you have an abundance of fruit and vegetables, freeze them in small portions and they're ready to go for your smoothies.

Powerful pumpkin seeds

These little seeds are really nutritious and, even in small servings they provide a significant amount of minerals, especially zinc and iron.

Berry Power

Serves: 1 | Prep: 15 mins | Cook: none

Per serving:	641 KCALS | 33.8G FAT | 3.7G SAT FAT | 72.7G CARBS | 41.8G SUGAR | 19.9G FIBRE | 22.1G PROTEIN | 0.1G SALT

Breakfast is arguably the most important meal of the day, and this shake includes lots of vital nutrients. It's quick to make, tasty and filling, but won't leave you feeling heavy.

Ingredients

20 g/¾ oz pumpkin seeds
20 g/¾ oz flaxseeds
20 g/¾ oz flaked almonds
115 g/4 oz raspberries
115 g/4 oz blueberries
225 g/8 oz vanilla soya yogurt
125 ml/4 fl oz chilled water

1. Put the pumpkin seeds, flaxseeds and almonds in a blender and blend until finely ground.

2. Add the raspberries, blueberries, yogurt and chilled water and blend until smooth.

3. Pour into a glass and serve.

Plum Power

Serves: 1 | Prep: 10–15 mins | Cook: 20 mins, plus cooling

Per serving: 289 KCALS | 3.6G FAT | 2.5G SAT FAT | 53.9G CARBS | 53.7G SUGAR | 2.1G FIBRE | 9.9G PROTEIN | 0.3G SALT

This pretty, icy fruit shake will cool you down while giving you a quick burst of energy from the plums and honey and more sustainable energy from the yogurt.

Ingredients

125 g/4½ oz plums, stoned
100 ml/3½ fl oz water
2 tsp clear honey
2 scoops natural frozen yogurt
1 Italian almond or pistachio biscotti, crumbled, to decorate (optional)
¼ plum, stoned, to decorate (optional)

1. Put the plums, water and honey into a small saucepan over a medium heat. Stir, cover tightly, reduce the heat to low and simmer for 15 minutes, until the plums have split and are very soft. Leave to cool.

2. Pour the mixture into a blender, then add the frozen yogurt and blend until smooth.

3. Pour into a glass, sprinkle over the biscotti, if using, decorate the rim with the plum, if using, and serve immediately.

Grape & Lychee Reviver

Serves: 1 | Prep: 15 mins | Cook: none

Per serving: 413 KCALS | 15.6G FAT | 2.3G SAT FAT | 72.8G CARBS | 54.6G SUGAR | 8.3G FIBRE | 6.2G PROTEIN | 0.1G SALT

Go oriental with fragrant lychees, thought by the Chinese to be the symbol of love. Blend them with creamy, smooth avocado and naturally sweet grapes for the perfect pick-me-up to rehydrate and fight fatigue.

Ingredients

300 g/10½ oz green grapes

55 g/2 oz young spinach

½ ripe avocado, stoned, flesh scooped from the skin

5 lychees, peeled and stoned

small handful of crushed ice

125 ml/4 fl oz chilled water

1 slice of avocado to serve (optional)

1. Feed the grapes and spinach through a juicer.

2. Pour the juice into a blender, add the avocado, lychees and crushed ice, and blend until smooth.

3. Add the water and blend again. Pour into a glass, add the avocado slice, if using, and serve immediately.

Grape nutrition

Grapes are a good source of potassium, although weight for weight they provide only one-twentieth of the vitamin C of kiwi fruit.

Manuka Honey

Manuka honey is known for its immune boosting abilities and nutritional benefits. It slowly releases the glycogen that the body needs to function during sleep, promoting a deeper and more restful sleep. Heart disease, diabetes and arthritis are accentuated by a lack of proper rest, so incorporating Manuka honey within your diet can decrease these risks.

Vanilla, Almond & Banana Smoothie

Serves: 2 | Prep: 5 mins | Cook: none

Per serving: 330 KCALS | 18.1G FAT | 1.4G SAT FAT | 31.4G CARBS | 24.4G SUGAR | 6.4G FIBRE | 9.4G PROTEIN | 0.2G SALT

This protein-packed smoothie is sweetened only with dates, but it tastes as sweet and delicious as the best milkshake you've ever had.

Ingredients

225 ml/8 fl oz almond milk
60 g/2¼ oz almond butter
1 banana, peeled and roughly chopped
4 stoned dates
1 tsp vanilla extract
8–10 ice cubes

1. Place all the ingredients in a blender and blend until smooth.

2. Pour into two glasses and serve immediately.

Why not try?

Melon can be used instead of the pear or apple and will keep this juice cool and soothing.

Cucumber Soother

Serves: 1 | Prep: 10–15 mins | Cook: none

Per serving: 259 KCALS | 0.8G FAT | TRACE SAT FAT | 67.9G CARBS | 43.1G SUGAR | 3.2G FIBRE | 2.2G PROTEIN | TRACE SALT

This light, fresh-tasting juice made with the addition of soothing aloe vera gel can help to reduce digestive problems such as heartburn.

Ingredients

1 large pear, halved

100 g/3½ oz cucumber, roughly chopped

1 green apple, halved

10 g/¼ oz fresh mint

1 tbsp aloe vera gel

crushed ice, to serve (optional)

1 slice of cucumber, to garnish

1 fresh mint sprig, to garnish

1. Feed the pear, cucumber and apple, through a juicer with the mint.

2. Stir through the aloe vera gel until combined. Pour the crushed ice, if using, into a glass, then pour in the juice.

3. Serve immediately, garnished with a cucumber slice and a sprig of mint.

Stomach Soother

Serves: 1 | Prep: 15 mins | Cook: none

Per serving: 259 KCALS | 0.7G FAT | TRACE SAT FAT | 69.8G CARBS | 48.8G SUGAR | 2.2G FIBRE | 3.5G PROTEIN | TRACE SALT

Pineapple juice is great for improving digestion and soothing an upset tummy, and its effects are reinforced here with fresh ginger. The healing enzyme bromelain reduces bruising, so it can help with recovery from an injury.

Ingredients

½ sweet pineapple, peeled and cut into thick slices

1 lemon, zest and most of the pith removed, halved

2-cm/¾-inch piece fresh ginger, peeled

1 pineapple leaf, to decorate (optional)

1. Feed the pineapple, lemon and ginger through a juicer.

2. Pour into a glass, add the pineapple leaf as a stirrer, if using, and serve. Remove the pineapple leaf before drinking.

Turbo Recharger

Serves: 1 | Prep: 20 mins | Cook: none

Per serving: 413 KCALS | 3.8G FAT | 0.8G SAT FAT | 94.7G CARBS | 70.9G SUGAR | 10.2G FIBRE | 9.8G PROTEIN | 0.2G SALT

This smoothie includes everything you need to revitalize your body: rehydrating melon, energy-boosting banana, vitamin C-packed grapes and iron-rich watercress.

Ingredients

½ honeydew melon, peeled, deseeded and roughly chopped

1 banana, peeled and roughly chopped

1 kiwi fruit, peeled and roughly chopped

115 g/4 oz seedless green grapes

small handful of watercress

125 ml/4 fl oz unsweetened rice, almond or soya milk

small handful of crushed ice (optional)

1. Put the melon, banana, kiwi fruit, grapes and watercress in a blender and blend until smooth.

2. Add the milk and crushed ice, if using, and blend again, until smooth.

3. Pour into a glass and serve immediately.

Wow, watercress!

Watercress is packed with antioxidants, minerals and vitamins C and K. It's also rich in chlorophyll, which assists with the oxygenation of blood cells.

Go Nuts

Serves: 1 | Prep: 10–15 mins | Cook: none

Per serving: 546 KCALS | 32.1G FAT | 5.6G SAT FAT | 67.5G CARBS | 49.6G SUGAR | 14.9G FIBRE | 7.8G PROTEIN | 0.3G SALT

Smooth and creamy meets sweet and nutty in this delicious dairy-free pick-me-up. The addition of plump and juicy Medjool dates, grown on a tree known as 'the tree of life', lifts this smoothie right out of the ordinary.

Ingredients

½ avocado, stoned, flesh scooped from the skin
4 Brazil nuts
3 Medjool dates
10 g/¼ oz fresh ginger, peeled
350 ml/12 fl oz almond milk
¼ tsp ground cinnamon
crushed ice, to serve (optional)

1. Place the avocado, nuts, dates and ginger in a blender and blend until smooth and creamy.

2. Pour over the almond milk, add the cinnamon and blend again until smooth.

3. Pour the smoothie over crushed ice, if using, and serve immediately.

Cinnamon power

Cinnamon helps to regulate blood sugar, making it a great addition for diabetics and hypoglycaemics.

Bananas

Bananas are natural mood enhancers, rich in tryptophan, which the body converts into serotonin. This provokes a happier mood, soothing stress and relieving symptoms of PMS and SAD. Bananas are also antacids, lowering the distress associated with heartburn, stomach aches and acid reflux.

Sensational strawberries

Strawberries have more vitamin C than any other red berries and so have great antiviral and antibacterial properties. They are rich in beta carotene, which is converted by the body into vitamin A. Their natural fruit sugars also give the body an early-morning energy boost. They also contain lignin, which may help reduce blood cholesterol.

Berry Whip

Serves: 4 | Prep: 10–15 mins | Cook: none

Per serving: 213 KCALS | 12.8G FAT | 2.4G SAT FAT | 23.2G CARBS | 11.6G SUGAR | 3.5G FIBRE | 4.7G PROTEIN | 0.2G SALT

Frozen berries are a healthy and handy freezer staple. Here they're blitzed with protein-boosting cashew nuts and Brazil nuts for a delicious shake.

Ingredients

125 g/4½ oz frozen sliced strawberries
125 g/4½ oz frozen blueberries
40 g/1½ oz Brazil nuts
40 g/1½ oz cashew nut pieces
30 g/1 oz porridge oats
450 ml/16 fl oz almond milk
2 tbsp maple syrup

1. Place the strawberries, blueberries, Brazil nuts and cashew nut pieces in a blender. Sprinkle over the oats, then pour in half the almond milk. Blend until smooth.

2. Add the remaining milk and the maple syrup and blend until smooth.

3. Pour into four glasses and serve immediately with spoons. As the drink stands, the blueberries will almost set the liquid, but as soon as you stir it, it will turn to liquid again.

Berry Breakfast

Serves: 1 | Prep: 10 mins | Cook: none

Per serving: 290 KCALS | 5G FAT | 0.5G SAT FAT | 52.7G CARBS | 20.2G SUGAR | 14.6G FIBRE | 10.1G PROTEIN | TRACE SALT

This soothing breakfast-in-a-glass is packed with sustaining nutrients to keep up your energy levels all morning and see you through until lunchtime.

Ingredients

200 g/7 oz strawberries

100 g/3½ oz raspberries

100 ml/3½ fl oz unsweetened rice, almond or soya milk

40 g/1½ oz unsweetened muesli

1. Cut a strawberry in half and reserve one half to decorate. Hull the remaining strawberries.

2. Put the strawberries and raspberries in a blender and blend to a purée. Add the milk and muesli and blend again until almost smooth.

3. Pour into a glass, top with the reserved strawberry half and serve.

Why not try?

For another fruity option try papaya in place of the pineapple.

Pineapple Pump

Serves: 1 | Prep: 10–15 mins | Cook: none

Per serving: 233 KCALS | 2.1G FAT | 0.2G SAT FAT | 49.6G CARBS | 24.9G SUGAR | 4.8G FIBRE | 10.9G PROTEIN | 0.6G SALT

Protein- and mineral-rich wheatgrass really pumps up the nutrition in this vibrant green energizer. Celery, curly kale and pineapple will boost your intake of vitamins, minerals and fibre and will really get your digestive juices flowing.

Ingredients

5 celery sticks, roughly chopped

150 g/5½ oz curly green kale, shredded

150 g/5½ oz fresh pineapple, peeled, cored and roughly chopped

30 g/1 oz mint

1 tsp wheatgrass powder

1 small slice of fresh pineapple, to garnish

1 kale leaf, to garnish

1. Feed the celery, kale and pineapple through a juicer funnel with the mint.

2. Stir in the wheatgrass powder until combined.

3. Serve immediately, garnished with the slice of pineapple and a kale leaf.

Broccoli Booster

Serves: 1 | Prep: 10–15 mins | Cook: none

Per serving: 308 KCALS | 7.7G FAT | 1.7G SAT FAT | 56.8G CARBS | 31.9G SUGAR | 9.3G FIBRE | 13G PROTEIN | 0.2G SALT

Bananas suppress acid in the digestive tract, which alleviates heartburn and helps fight ulcers. They also contain a soluble fibre that aids the elimination process, so they are great for boosting digestive health.

Ingredients

150 g/5½ oz broccoli stem, roughly chopped

75 g/2¾ oz spinach

200 ml/7 fl oz chilled water

1 frozen banana

1 tbsp pumpkin seed butter

1 tbsp manuka honey

1. Put the broccoli in a blender with the spinach and water and blend until smooth.

2. Add the banana, pumpkin seed butter and honey, and blend again until smooth and creamy. Serve immediately.

Seed butter

There are lots of seed butters to try, all with great benefits, so look out for sesame, hemp and pumpkin butters.

Beat the Morning Blues

Serves: 1 | Prep: 10–15 mins | Cook: none

Per serving: 294 KCALS | 5.3G FAT | 0.4G SAT FAT | 62G CARBS | 40.4G SUGAR | 5.9G FIBRE | 5.4G PROTEIN | TRACE SALT

Full of vitamin C-packed, antioxidant-rich delicious blueberries, this hearty non-dairy juice is a truly supercharged breakfast immunity boost!

Ingredients

1 pear, halved
150 g/5½ oz blueberries
100 ml/3½ fl oz soya yogurt
½ tsp agave syrup
2 tsp flaked almonds, toasted

1. Feed the pear through a juicer. Pour the juice into a blender, add the blueberries and blend until smooth.

2. Add the yogurt and agave syrup and blend until smooth.

3. Pour into a glass, sprinkle with the almonds and serve.

Cleanse your body and introduce juices like Big Apple Detox, Fennel Flush, Green Tea Punch and Spinach Aid to help you feel revitalized, toxin-free and healthy. The recipes in this chapter are not just super-tasty but they will provide essential carbohydrates, fibre, plant chemicals and plenty of vitamin C to help us feel like we're running at optimum efficiency.

DETOX

Pine-nettle Smoothie

Serves: 2 | Prep: 15–20 mins | Cook: none

Per serving: 351 KCALS | 2.4G FAT | 0.2G SAT FAT | 83.1G CARBS | 53.1G SUGAR | 12.8G FIBRE | 6.9G PROTEIN | TRACE SALT

Nettles are said to help purify the blood – they're certainly rich in iron – and consuming them with fruits such as pineapple and lemon that contain vitamin C helps the body to absorb this important mineral.

Ingredients

Nettle layer

100 g/3½ oz nettle leaves, rinsed and blanched

1 apple, cored and roughly chopped

1 lemon, peeled and roughly chopped

2 stoned dates, quartered

¼ tsp dried ginger

100 ml/3½ fl oz orange juice

Pineapple layer

450 g/1 lb fresh pineapple, peeled and cored

100 ml/3½ fl oz soya yogurt

30 g/1 oz rolled oats

1. To make the nettle layer, put all the ingredients into a blender and blend until smooth. Transfer to a jug and rinse the blender goblet.

2. To make the pineapple layer, chop the pineapple into bite-sized pieces. Place in the blender, add the yogurt and oats and blend until smooth.

3. Layer the two mixtures in two large glasses and serve immediately.

Nutritious nettles

Once they're steamed and blended, nettles can't sting you – but handle with care before you steam them! The stinging barbs are on the stems and the underside of the leaves.

Parsley Purifier

Serves: 1 | Prep: 10–15 mins | Cook: none

Per serving: 152 KCALS | 2.5G FAT | 0.2G SAT FAT | 22.1G CARBS | 9.7G SUGAR | 1.9G FIBRE | 7G PROTEIN | 0.3G SALT

As a diuretic, this drink really helps to cleanse your body. The strong flavours of the herbs and garlic are balanced by the natural sweetness of the sugar snap peas and the delicate flavour of the cucumber.

Ingredients

115 g/4 oz sugar snap peas
small handful of fresh flat-leaf parsley
2 fresh rosemary sprigs
1 garlic clove
55 g/2 oz young spinach
½ cucumber
2 celery sticks, halved
1 tsp hempseed oil
chilled water, to taste
ice cubes, to serve (optional)

1. Feed the peas, parsley (reserving 1 sprig to garnish), rosemary and garlic through a juicer, followed by the spinach, cucumber and celery.

2. Pour into a glass and stir in the oil with water to taste.

3. Garnish with the reserved parsley sprig and serve with ice, if using.

Take a fresh look at parsley

Parsley is rich in calcium and potassium too, and has lots of iron and phosphorus. Just 2 tablespoons of parsley contains a whopping 153 per cent of the recommended daily allowance of vitamin K (which works with protein to strengthen bones).

Big Apple Detox

Serves: 1 | Prep: 10 mins | Cook: none

Per serving: 302 KCALS | 1G FAT | 0.2G SAT FAT | 77.5G CARBS | 45G SUGAR | 4G FIBRE | 2.7G PROTEIN | TRACE SALT

With its creamy, delicate parsnip and apple flavour fortified with cleansing ginger, this juice is perfect after an indulgent holiday or Christmas.

Ingredients

1 parsnip, halved
5-mm/¼-inch piece of fresh ginger, peeled
2 apples, halved
125 ml/4 fl oz chilled water
small handful of crushed ice (optional)

1. Feed the parsnip and ginger, then the apples through a juicer. Top up with the water.

2. Half-fill a glass with crushed ice, if using, then pour in the juice and serve immediately.

Fresh is best

Instead of buying commercially made detox compounds or potions, juice fresh fruit and vegetables at home. Look at what you eat and when; you might find that making small changes will have a big impact. Ditch that high-calorie, full-fat coffee latte or cola and have a low-calorie, high-vitamin and high-mineral juice instead.

Broccoli & Parsley Revitalizer

Serves: 1 | Prep: 10–15 mins | Cook: none

Per serving: 119 KCALS | 0.6G FAT | 0G SAT FAT | 27G CARBS | 15.1G SUGAR | 0.2G FIBRE | 3.2G PROTEIN | 0.2G SALT

Ingredients

115 g/4 oz broccoli, broken into large florets

small handful of fresh flat-leaf parsley

½ fennel bulb

2 apples, halved

chilled water, to taste

handful of crushed ice (optional)

1. Feed the broccoli and parsley, then the fennel and apples through a juicer. Add water to taste.

2. Half-fill a glass with crushed ice, if using, pour in the juice and serve immediately.

Papaya & Apricot Soother

Serves: 1 | Prep: 15–20 mins | Cook: none

Per serving: 220 KCALS | 1.3G FAT | 0.1G SAT FAT | 53.3G CARBS | 39.7G SUGAR | 6G FIBRE | 4.1G PROTEIN | TRACE SALT

Ingredients

½ papaya, peeled, deseeded and roughly chopped

4 apricots, halved and stoned

juice of 2 oranges

juice of 1 lime

small handful of crushed ice (optional)

4 tbsp chilled water

1. Put the papaya, apricots, orange juice and lime juice in a blender and blend until smooth.

2. Add the crushed ice, if using, and water and blend again until smooth.

3. Pour into a glass and serve immediately.

Why not try?

Celery is a good substitute for fennel but you will lose the delicate aniseed flavour.

Fennel Flush

Serves: 1 | Prep: 10–15 mins | Cook: none

Per serving: 225 KCALS | 1.5G FAT | 0.3G SAT FAT | 55.9G CARBS | 29.6G SUGAR | 4.3G FIBRE | 7.4G PROTEIN | 0.5G SALT

Fennel is a great source of fibre and contains potent antioxidants, which have been shown to reduce inflammation. Taking care of your insides will soon have you glowing on the outside.

Ingredients

100 g/3½ oz spinach

20 g/¾ oz fresh mint

1 large fennel bulb, roughly chopped

1 green apple, halved

1 lime, zest and pith removed, deseeded and roughly chopped

crushed ice, to serve (optional)

1. Feed the spinach, mint, fennel, apple and lime through a juicer.

2. Stir well and pour over the crushed ice, if using. Serve immediately.

Nettles

Nettles can sting (blanching in boiling water for a minute is one way to remove the sting), but including them in your diet will add valuable nutritional benefits. They are naturally high in iron, aiding red blood cell production for fending off diseases and infections, also benefiting hair, skin and nail health. Nettles are also incredibly high in calcium, promoting strong teeth and bones.

Green Jump Start

Serves: 1 | Prep: 10 mins | Cook: none

Per serving: 223 KCALS | 1.3G FAT | TRACE SAT FAT | 51.4G CARBS | 35.6G SUGAR | 1G FIBRE | 6.4G PROTEIN | 0.1 SALT

You don't get a huge amount of juice from these green leaves, but what you do get is concentrated with antioxidants, minerals and vitamins. Mix them with courgettes and apples for a health boost that will jump-start your detox.

Ingredients

55 g/2 oz young spinach
30 g/1 oz watercress
1 courgette, halved
2 apples, halved
1 tsp wheatgrass powder (optional)
small handful of crushed ice (optional)

1. Feed the spinach and watercress, then the courgette and apples through a juicer.

2. Stir in the wheatgrass powder, if using.

3. Half-fill a glass with crushed ice, if using, then pour in the juice and serve immediately.

Get into good habits

A detox can help you review your eating habits. Most of us don't eat enough green veg, and this tasty juice is a way to increase your consumption easily.

Bright Eyes

Serves: 1 | Prep: 15 mins, plus cooling | Cook: none

Per serving: 124 KCALS | 0.5G FAT | TRACE SAT FAT | 31.4G CARBS | 21.9G SUGAR | 6.5G FIBRE | 1.5G PROTEIN | 0.1G SALT

Put a sparkle in your eyes with this delicious juice that contains cleansing and antioxidant-rich green tea, carrot, apple and parsley. Green tea and parsley are also thought to help improve ageing eyesight.

Ingredients

100 ml/3½ fl oz boiling water

1 green tea sachet, or 1 tsp green tea

1 carrot, roughly chopped

1 apple, halved

small handful of fresh flat-leaf parsley

1–2 fresh flat-leaf parsley sprigs, to garnish

1. Pour the boiling water onto the green tea and leave to stand for 4 minutes. Strain and leave to cool slightly.

2. Put the carrot, apple and parsley into a food processor or blender and process until smooth. Stir the juice into the tea.

3. Pour into a glass and serve warm or cold, garnished with parsley.

Green Tea Punch

Serves: 1 | Prep: 10–15 mins | Cook: none

Per serving: 62 KCALS | 0.6G FAT | TRACE SAT FAT | 7.6G CARBS | 0.7G SUGAR | 2.6G FIBRE | 6.8G PROTEIN | TRACE SALT

Green tea is packed with antioxidants. Combined with ginseng and wheatgrass, this is a great detoxifying juice that will cleanse you from the inside out.

Ingredients

300 ml/10 fl oz green tea
juice of ½ lemon
¼ tsp liquid ginseng
1 tsp pea protein
1 tsp wheatgrass powder
1 tsp maca powder
ice cubes, to serve

1. Whisk the green tea with the lemon juice, ginseng, pea protein, wheatgrass powder and maca powder. Alternatively, you could combine the ingredients in a blender.

2. Serve immediately over ice.

Beet Aid Detox

Serves: 1 | Prep: 10 mins | Cook: none

Per serving: 216 KCALS | 1.1G FAT | 0.1G SAT FAT | 53.1G CARBS | 40.2G SUGAR | 5.9G FIBRE | 5.9G PROTEIN | 0.5G SALT

This ruby-red juice looks more like a summer cocktail than an aid to detox! The inclusion of red chard boosts the antioxidant properties of its near relative, luscious beetroot, and the lime juice adds a zesty touch.

Ingredients

1 beetroot, halved

½ lime, zest and pith removed, deseeded and roughly chopped

55 g/2 oz red chard

675 g/1 lb 8 oz watermelon, thickly sliced and peeled

small handful of crushed ice (optional)

1. Feed the beetroot and the lime, then the chard and watermelon through a juicer.

2. Half-fill a glass with crushed ice, if using, then pour in the juice and serve immediately.

Health notes

Beetroot contains almost all the vitamins and minerals needed to give your whole body a boost. Watermelon's high water content helps to rehydrate and plump up your skin.

Why not try?

If you don't like celery, or just want to try something different, replace it with cucumber.

Rapid Recharge

Serves: 1 | Prep: 15 mins | Cook: none

Per serving: 200 KCALS | 1.3G FAT | 0.2G SAT FAT | 48.3G CARBS | 36.4G SUGAR | 7.7G FIBRE | 5.3G PROTEIN | 0.2G SALT

Alfalfa sprouts contain high concentrations of calcium, vitamin K and vitamin C, and give a great nutritional boost to this fresh-looking, cleansing green juice.

Ingredients

1 small courgette, halved
1 celery stick, roughly chopped
40 g/1½ oz baby leaf spinach
40 g/1½ oz alfalfa sprouts
2 apples, peeled and cored
1 tsp alfalfa sprouts, to garnish

1. Put the courgette in a blender with the celery. Add the spinach and the alfalfa sprouts, then the apples.

2. Blend all the ingredients together, then pour into a glass.

3. Garnish with a few alfalfa sprouts and serve.

Fabulous fennel

Fennel acts as a diuretic and has a calming effect on the stomach while providing useful amounts of beta-carotene and folate.

Red Cabbage Digestive Aid

Serves: 1 | Prep: 15 mins | Cook: none

Per serving: 211 KCALS | 0.8G FAT | 0.2G SAT FAT | 52.5G CARBS | 35.8G SUGAR | 2.9G FIBRE | 5.7G PROTEIN | 0.3G SALT

You will be amazed at the vibrant purple juice that comes from a red cabbage. This drink is light and aromatic, with a hint of cardamom (said to calm digestion) and the delicate sweetness of red grapes.

Ingredients

150 g/5½ oz red grapes
½ fennel bulb
¼ head of red cabbage, roughly chopped
3 cardamom pods
chilled water, to taste
small handful of crushed ice (optional)

1. Feed the grapes, then the fennel, then the cabbage through a juicer.

2. Roughly crush the cardamom in a mortar with a pestle, discard the pods and then finely crush the black seeds and stir them into the juice. Top up with water to taste.

3. Half-fill a glass with crushed ice, if using, then pour in the juice and serve immediately.

Mother Earth
Coconut Restorer

Mother Earth

Serves: 1 | Prep: 10–15 mins | Cook: none

Per serving: 248 KCALS | 15.7G FAT | 2.3G SAT FAT | 24.9G CARBS | 11G SUGAR | 10.6G FIBRE | 5.5G PROTEIN | 0.2G SALT

Ingredients

30 g/1 oz curly green kale
300 ml/10 fl oz chilled water
2 celery sticks, roughly chopped
½ avocado, halved, stoned, flesh scooped from skin
1 small piece turmeric root, peeled
1 tbsp yuzu juice
2.5-cm/1-inch piece fresh ginger, peeled
1 tsp bee pollen
1 tbsp goji berries

1. Shred the kale and put in a blender with the water and blend until smooth.

2. Chop the celery and avocado and add to the blender with the turmeric, yuzu juice, ginger, bee pollen and goji berries.

3. Blend until smooth and serve immediately.

Coconut Restorer

Serves: 1 | Prep: 10–15 mins | Cook: none

Per serving: 162 KCALS | 11.7G FAT | 4.4G SAT FAT | 11.4G CARBS | 4.5G SUGAR | 4.8G FIBRE | 5.1G PROTEIN | 0.3G SALT

Ingredients

30 g/1 oz cavolo nero
20 g/¾ oz beetroot leaves
1 tsp chia seeds
2 tsp almond butter
200 ml/7 fl oz coconut milk
125 ml/4 fl oz chilled water
pinch of chia seeds, to garnish

1. Shred the cavolo nero and put into a blender with the beetroot leaves, chia seeds and almond butter.

2. Pour over the coconut milk and water, and blend until smooth and creamy.

3. Serve immediately, sprinkled with chia seeds.

Green Tea

Green tea is known for containing a higher concentration of vitamins than other food and drink, making it incredibly valuable for the body. It contains more than five times the amount of folic acid found in spinach, which is proven to decrease the risks of colon cancer and dementia. It also contains elements of GABA, an acid that contributes to the lowering of blood pressure.

Healing turmeric

Turmeric, a relation of ginger, has long been used in Chinese medicine to help treat depression. It is a natural antiseptic and anti-bacterial agent. However, it's the anti-inflammatory properties that may be of the most interest – they may help arthritis sufferers, soothe inflammatory skin infections such as psoriasis, and according to one study help reduce the incidence of Alzheimer's Disease.

Nature's Remedy

Serves: 1 | Prep: 10–15 mins | Cook: none

Per serving: 252 KCALS | 0.8G FAT | 0.1G SAT FAT | 60.4G CARBS | 27.3G SUGAR | 3.8G FIBRE | 4.9G PROTEIN | 0.2G SALT

This drink tastes surprisingly mild, with a natural sweetness from the parsnip and carrots, and boy-oh-boy does it do you good!

Ingredients

2 carrots, halved
½ small onion, halved
1 garlic clove
1 parsnip, halved
1 orange, zest and a little pith removed, halved
50 ml/2 fl oz chilled water
pinch of ground turmeric
pinch of pepper
small handful of crushed ice (optional)

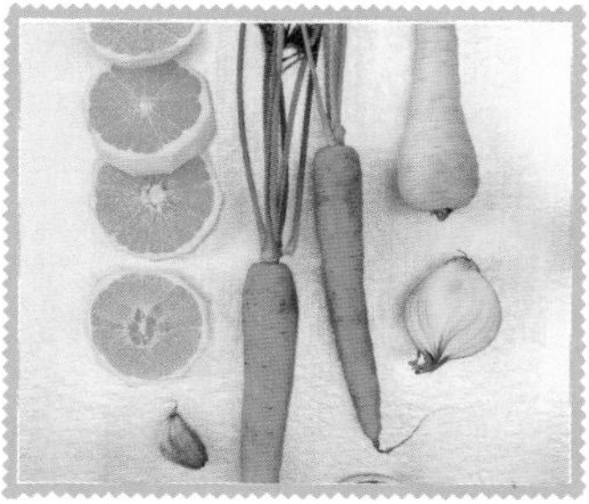

1. Cut a thin slice from a carrot and reserve.

2. Feed the remaining carrots and the onion, garlic and parsnip, then the orange through a juicer. Stir in the water, turmeric and pepper.

3. Half-fill a glass with crushed ice, if using, pour in the juice, garnish with the carrot slice and serve.

Stress Buster

Serves: 1 | Prep: 15 mins | Cook: none

Per serving: 48 KCALS | 0.3G FAT | 0G SAT FAT | 10.4G CARBS | 7.6G SUGAR | 0.1G FIBRE | 1.1G PROTEIN | TRACE SALT

Ginseng is a natural stimulant that helps to combat stress and lifts the mood. This teatime juice also aids liver and kidney function and prevents fluid retention.

Ingredients

1 ginseng tea bag or 1 tsp ginseng tea

150 ml/5 fl oz boiling water

1 apple, halved

40 g/1½ oz rocket leaves

1. Put the tea in a cup, pour over the boiling water and leave to stand for 4 minutes. Strain the water into a glass.

2. Feed the apple and then the rocket through a juicer.

3. Stir the juice into the tea and serve warm or cold.

Dandelion Sunrise

Serves: 1 | Prep: 10–15 mins | Cook: none

Per serving: 287 KCALS | 23G FAT | 7.9G SAT FAT | 16G CARBS | 3G SUGAR | 4.3G FIBRE | 9.3G PROTEIN | TRACE SALT

Coconut butter is a spread made from the flesh of the coconut in the same way that peanuts are used to make peanut butter. It's packed with healthy fats and helps to keep you fuller for longer when added to smoothies.

Ingredients

30 g/1 oz dandelion leaves
55 g/2 oz curly green kale, shredded
200 ml/7 fl oz chilled water
30 g/1 oz cashew nuts
½ tbsp coconut butter
1 tbsp sunflower seeds

1. Put the dandelion leaves into a blender with the kale and water and blend until smooth.

2. Add the cashew nuts, coconut butter and sunflower seeds and blend until smooth and creamy. Serve immediately.

Why not try?

Add 1 teaspoon of barleygrass to help rid the body of toxins. Almonds or macadamia nuts would also work well in this recipe.

Green Goddess

Serves: 1 | Prep: 15 mins | Cook: none

Per serving: 71 KCALS | 0.5G FAT | 0G SAT FAT | 14.3G CARBS | 11.5G SUGAR | 0.6G FIBRE | 2.2G PROTEIN | 0.2G SALT

This cooling, cleansing drink is good for liver and kidney function, helps lower cholesterol and relieves tension and insomnia. It's high in iron and chlorophyll, which benefits your eyes and helps maintain healthy blood vessels.

Ingredients

½ Galia melon, thickly sliced and peeled

85 g/3 oz young spinach

2 large fresh flat-leaf parsley sprigs

3 large fresh mint sprigs

small handful of crushed ice (optional)

1. Feed the melon, then the spinach, then the parsley and 2 mint sprigs through a juicer.

2. Half-fill a glass with crushed ice, if using, then pour in the juice.

3. Garnish with the remaining mint sprig and serve immediately.

Added extras

Add a little frozen mango to this shot to brighten the flavour and help the medicine go down!

Spinach Aid

Serves: 1 | Prep: 10–15 mins | Cook: none

Per serving: 23 KCALS | 0.2G FAT | TRACE SAT FAT | 5.2G CARBS | 0.4G SUGAR | 0.5G FIBRE | 1.3G PROTEIN | TRACE SALT

Dark and dreamy, this vibrant green shot packs a super-charge of goodness – for maximum benefit, don't leave a single drop in the glass!

Ingredients

20 g/¾ oz spinach
1 tbsp aloe vera gel
juice of ½ lime
½ tsp spirulina powder
3½ tbsp chilled water

1. Place the spinach, aloe vera, lime juice and spirulina powder in a blender.
2. Pour in the water and blend until smooth. Serve immediately.

Index